Editor

Cristina Krysinski, M. Ed.

Editor in Chief

Karen J. Goldfluss, M.S. Ed.

Creative Director

Sarah M. Smith

Cover Artist

Brenda DiAntonis

Art Coordinator

Renée McElwee

Illustrator

Amanda R. Harter

Imaging

Amanda R. Harter

Publisher

Mary D. Smith, M.S. Ed.

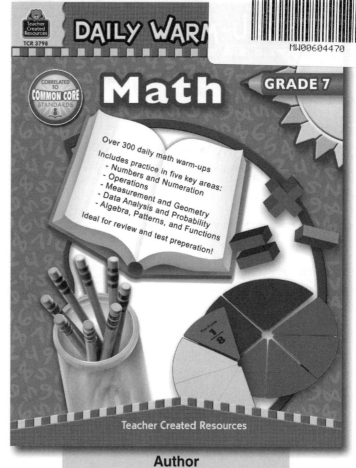

DAILY WARM-UPS

Math

GRADE 7

TCR 3798

CORRELATED TO COMMON CORE STANDARDS

Over 300 daily math warm-ups
Includes practice in five key areas:
- Numbers and Numeration
- Operations
- Measurement and Geometry
- Data Analysis and Probability
- Algebra, Patterns, and Functions
Ideal for review and test preperation!

Teacher Created Resources

Author

Heath Roddy

CORRELATED TO COMMON CORE STANDARDS

For correlations to the Common Core State Standards please visit *http://www.teachercreated.com/standards.*

Teacher Created Resources

6421 Industry Way
Westminster, CA 92683
www.teachercreated.com

ISBN: 978-1-4206-3798-4

© *2014 Teacher Created Resources*
Made in U.S.A.

Teacher Created Resources

The *Daily Warm-Ups: Math* series was written to provide students with frequent opportunities to master and retain important math skills. The unique format used in this series provides students with the opportunity to improve their own fluency in math. Each Daily Warm-Up includes two warm-ups that take the form of either multiple-choice, fill-in, or writing the answer on the line provided. For the multiple-choice questions, students are to mark the bubble corresponding to the answer they chose. Each section consists of over 30 pages of challenging problems that meet Common Core State Standards. (See Table of Contents to find a listing of specific subject areas. Answer keys are located at the back of each section.) Use the tracking sheet on page 6 to record which warm-up exercises you have given to your students. Or, distribute copies of the sheet for students to keep their own record.

This book is divided into five sections. The sections are as follows:

- Numbers and Numeration
- Operations
- Measurement and Geometry
- Data Analysis and Probability
- Algebra, Patterns, and Functions

Daily Warm-Ups: Math gives students a year-long collection of challenging problems to reinforce key math skills taught in the classroom. As students become active learners in discovering mathematical relationships, they acquire a necessary understanding that improves their problem-solving skills and, therefore, boosts their confidence in math. When using this book, keep the idea of incorporating the warm-ups with the actual curriculum that you may be currently using in your classroom. This provides students with a greater chance of mastering the math skills.

This book can be used in a variety of ways. However, the exercises in this book were designed to be used as warm-ups where students will have the opportunity to work problems and obtain immediate feedback from their teacher. To help ensure student success, spend a few moments each day discussing problems and solutions. This extra time will not take very long and will yield great results from students! As you use this book, you will be excited to watch your students discover how exciting math concepts can be!

Teaching Tips

Ideas on how to use the warm-ups are as follows:

- *Discussion*—Most warm-ups can be completed in a short amount of time. When time is up, model how to correctly work the problems. You may wish to have students correct their own work. Allow time for students to discuss problems and their solutions to problems. You may want to allow students the opportunity to discuss their answers or the way they solved the problems with partners. Discuss why some answers are correct and why others are not. Students should be able to support their choices. Having students understand that there are many ways of approaching a problem and strategies used in dealing with them are a great benefit for all students. The time you allow students to do this is just as important as the time spent completing the problems.

- *Review*—Give students the warm-up at the end of the lesson as a means of tying in an objective taught that day. The problems students encounter on each warm-up are designed to improve math fluency and are not intended to be included as a math grade. If the student has difficulty with an objective, review the material again with him or her independently and provide additional instruction.

Teaching Tips (cont.)

- *Assessment*—The warm-ups can be used as a preliminary assessment to find out what your students know. Use the assessment to tailor your lessons.
- *Introduction*—Use the warm-ups as an introduction into the new objective to be taught. Select warm-ups according to the specific skill or skills to be introduced. The warm-ups do not have to be distributed in any particular order.
- *Independent Work*—Photocopy the warm-up for students to work on independently.
- *Model*—Invite students to come to the board to model how they approached a problem on the warm-up.
- *Test Preparation*—The warm-ups can be a great way to prepare for math tests in the classroom or for any standardized testing. You may wish to select warm-ups from all sections to use as practice tests and/or review prior to standardized testing.

Student Tips

Below is a chart that you may photocopy and cut out for each student. It will give students a variety of strategies to use when dealing with difficult problems.

Math Tips

✓ Write word problems as number problems.

✓ Underline the question and circle any key words.

✓ Make educated guesses when you encounter multiple-choice problems or problems with which you are not familiar.

✓ Leave harder problems for last. Then, come back to solve those problems after you have completed all other problems on the warm-up.

✓ Use items or problem-solving strategies, such as drawing a diagram or making a table, to solve the problem.

✓ Always check your answer to see that it makes sense.

Numbers and Numeration Warm-Ups

1		8		15		22		29		36		43		50		57	
2		9		16		23		30		37		44		51		58	
3		10		17		24		31		38		45		52		59	
4		11		18		25		32		39		46		53		60	
5		12		19		26		33		40		47		54		61	
6		13		20		27		34		41		48		55		62	
7		14		21		28		35		42		49		56			

Operations Warm-Ups

1		8		15		22		29		36		43		50		57	
2		9		16		23		30		37		44		51		58	
3		10		17		24		31		38		45		52		59	
4		11		18		25		32		39		46		53		60	
5		12		19		26		33		40		47		54		61	
6		13		20		27		34		41		48		55		62	
7		14		21		28		35		42		49		56			

Measurement and Geometry Warm-Ups

1		8		15		22		29		36		43		50		57	
2		9		16		23		30		37		44		51		58	
3		10		17		24		31		38		45		52		59	
4		11		18		25		32		39		46		53		60	
5		12		19		26		33		40		47		54		61	
6		13		20		27		34		41		48		55		62	
7		14		21		28		35		42		49		56			

Data Analysis and Probability Warm-Ups

1		8		15		22		29		36		43		50		57	
2		9		16		23		30		37		44		51		58	
3		10		17		24		31		38		45		52		59	
4		11		18		25		32		39		46		53		60	
5		12		19		26		33		40		47		54		61	
6		13		20		27		34		41		48		55		62	
7		14		21		28		35		42		49		56			

Algebra, Patterns, and Functions Warm-Ups

1		8		15		22		29		36		43		50		57	
2		9		16		23		30		37		44		51		58	
3		10		17		24		31		38		45		52		59	
4		11		18		25		32		39		46		53		60	
5		12		19		26		33		40		47		54		61	
6		13		20		27		34		41		48		55		62	
7		14		21		28		35		42		49		56			

Numbers and Numeration

Name

1. Kristi and David are driving from East Bernard, Texas, to Florida to take their children on vacation. After driving 11 hours, they had driven 605 miles. What was their average speed in miles per hour?

Answer: _____

2. Mr. Robins is ordering art supplies for his students. He needs 3 pints of paint to do 2 projects. How many pints of paint will Mr. Robins need for each project?

Answer: _____

Name

1. Robin needs a piece of rope to make a swing for her son. The hardware store sells 3-foot lengths of rope for $6.30 each. Find the cost of the rope per foot.

Answer: _____

2. Chandler answered 22 out of 25 questions correctly on his quiz. What percentage of the quiz questions did he answer correctly?

Answer: _____

Name

1. Simplify the expression: $(5 \times 7 + 3) - 8 \div 4$.

Answer: _____

2. James's truck shows that his average gas mileage per day is 29 miles per gallon of gas. If James drives about 87 miles each day, about how much gas does he use in 14 days of driving?

Answer: _____

Name

1. At the Wharton Junior High Concert, 35% of the people attending the concert are 7th graders. What fraction of the people attending the concert are 7th graders? Reduce the fraction to lowest terms.

Answer: _____

2. Hank wrote the numbers below on the whiteboard.

0.237	$\frac{1}{4}$	24%

Which of these rational numbers is the greatest? _____

Which of these rational numbers is the least? _____

Name

1. Place the following values in order from greatest to least.

72%   0.713 $\frac{3}{4}$ $\frac{2}{3}$

_____   _____   _____   _____

2. The table below shows the time in minutes that it took four students to put together a puzzle. In what order did the students complete their puzzle?

Student	Time in Minutes
Sarah	$7\frac{3}{4}$
Richard	7.23
Brenda	$7\frac{1}{2}$
Teresa	8.2

1st

_____

2nd

_____

3rd

_____

4th

_____

Name

1. Sandra is making a snack mix for her children. The ingredients are listed below.

Ingredients

$1\frac{1}{4}$ cups of raisins	$\frac{1}{2}$ cup of chocolate chunks	$1\frac{1}{4}$ cups of pretzels
$\frac{3}{4}$ cup of almonds	$\frac{1}{4}$ cup of dried blueberries	$\frac{1}{2}$ cup of granola

What is the total amount of all six ingredients?

Ⓐ $3\frac{1}{4}$ cups   Ⓑ 4 cups   Ⓒ $4\frac{1}{2}$ cups   Ⓓ $4\frac{3}{4}$ cups

2. Find the **greatest common factor** for each set of numbers.

A. 12 and 18   **B.** 24, 36, and 48

_____   _____

Name

1. What is the **greatest common factor** for each set of numbers?

   A. 15 and 20 _____

   B. 28, 16, and 32 _____

   C. 21 and 63 _____

   D. 24, 40, and 64 _____

2. Write these scientific notation values in standard form:

   A. 3.9×10^4 _____

   B. 6.7×10^{-5} _____

   C. 9.8×10^7 _____

Name

1. Write <, >, or = to make the statement true.

$$4.08 \times 10^3 \quad \bigcirc \quad 4.08 \times 10^4$$

2. At the start of a new school year, Mrs. Brooks had 20 students in her class. Of the 20 students, there were 11 girls. What is the ratio of boys to girls in Mrs. Brooks's class?

   Ⓐ 11:20

   Ⓑ 9:11

   Ⓒ 11:9

   Ⓓ 9:20

Name

1. Mrs. Dornak wrote the number 833,000 on the board. She asked Sheri to come to the board and write the number using scientific notation. If Sheri wrote it correctly, which answer choice below did she write on the board?

Ⓐ 800,000 + 33,000

Ⓒ 833×10^5

Ⓑ 8.33×10^5

Ⓓ $(8 \times 100,000) + (33 \times 10,000)$

2. Which number is equivalent to the following scientific notation value?

$$5.048 \times 10^{-2} \text{ cm}$$

Ⓐ 504,800 cm

Ⓒ 0.005048 cm

Ⓑ 504.8 cm

Ⓓ 0.05048 cm

Name

1. Use the models below to find the square root equations.

A.

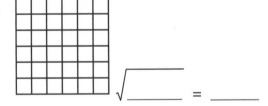

B.

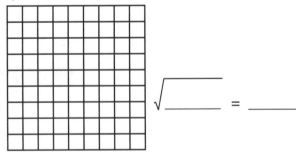

2. Fill in the missing blanks in the chart below.

Fraction	Decimal	Percent
$\frac{1}{2}$	0.5	
$\frac{1}{4}$		25%
	0.2	20%
$\frac{2}{5}$	0.4	

Name

1. At Jordan Junior High, students sent a survey to parents asking what type of vacation spots they would most likely visit with their families during summer break. Of the 250 parents that responded, how many parents chose camping as their most likely destination?

Ⓐ 32 parents

Ⓒ 80 parents

Ⓑ 45 parents

Ⓓ 170 parents

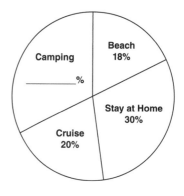

2. Rewrite 48% as a fraction. _____

Simplify your answer

Rewrite 225% as a mixed number. _____

Simplify your answer

Name

1. Christi found 14 pennies, 5 quarters, and 6 dimes in the bottom of her purse. Write the ratio of dimes found to total coins found as a decimal.

Answer: _____

2. Look at the table below. Which color of candy does Mary have the least amount of?

Blue and Red Candy	
Blue Jelly Beans	$\frac{7}{8}$
Red Jelly Beans	$\frac{2}{3}$
Blue Gummy Bears	$\frac{7}{8}$
Red Gummy Bears	$\frac{3}{4}$

Answer: _____

1. At Benton Appliances, washing machines are on sale for 30% off the original price. Tammy found a coupon in the newspaper for an additional 18% discount off the sale price. If the original price of the washing machine is $500, how much will Tammy pay for the washing machine before tax?

Answer: _____

2. A teacher is polling her class of 30 students to find how they get to school each morning. The table below shows the results. According to the table, how many students arrive by bus?

Ⓐ 4 students

Ⓑ 10 students

Ⓒ 14 students

Ⓓ 6 students

Transportation	Number of Students
Bike	$\frac{1}{5}$
Car	$\frac{1}{3}$
Bus	?

1. Jake, Sam, Kyle, and Mark were each told to write an example of an irrational number. Whose example is correct?

Ⓐ
Jake
Square root of 5

Ⓑ
Sam
Square root of 9

Ⓒ
Kyle
-1

Ⓓ
Mark
$-\frac{2}{3}$

2. Derek is buying a gift for his sister's birthday. The original price of the gift is $12.99, and it is on sale for $\frac{1}{4}$ off. Write an expression that Derek can use to find the discount. How much will Derek pay for the gift before tax?

Answer: _____

Name

1. The table below shows the set of fractions that four friends wrote on the board. The goal was to place the fractions in order from least to greatest. Which friend did this correctly?

Ⓐ Tammy

Ⓑ Tracey

Ⓒ Maci

Ⓓ Kendall

Friend	Fraction
Tammy	$\frac{5}{6}, \frac{1}{4}, \frac{3}{4}, \frac{2}{3}$
Tracey	$\frac{5}{6}, \frac{1}{4}, \frac{2}{3}, \frac{3}{4}$
Maci	$\frac{2}{3}, \frac{3}{4}, \frac{1}{4}, \frac{5}{6}$
Kendall	$\frac{1}{4}, \frac{2}{3}, \frac{3}{4}, \frac{5}{6}$

2. Michael scored 549,457,839 points playing a video game. Josh scored 538,457,839 points on the same game. Which place value is important in determining who earned the higher score?

Ⓐ hundred millions

Ⓒ millions

Ⓑ ten millions

Ⓓ hundred thousands

Name

1. Look at the number below. How will the value of the number change if the digit 1 is replaced by a 9?

$$532,084,167$$

Ⓐ The ten millions place will increase by 80,000,000.

Ⓑ The millions place will increase by 8,000,000.

Ⓒ The hundreds place will increase by 800.

Ⓓ The hundred thousands place will increase by 800,000.

2. The teacher wrote the decimal 3.08 on the board. She asked four students what fraction is equivalent to this number. The chart shows their answers. Which student got the correct answer?

Ⓐ Dwayne

Ⓒ Terry

Ⓑ Robin

Ⓓ James

Student	Answer
James	$\frac{56}{25}$
Terry	$\frac{77}{25}$
Robin	$\frac{19}{5}$
Dwayne	$\frac{32}{5}$

Name

1. Austin wrote the number shown below. Heath wrote a number slightly less than half of the number Austin wrote. What number below is **approximately** the number Heath wrote?

> **Austin's Number: 7.3×10^6**

Ⓐ 17,700,000

Ⓒ 3,500,000

Ⓑ 3,900,000

Ⓓ 135,000

2. A group of 10 students will stay after school in Mrs. Watkins's class for tutoring. Four students will practice math on the computer, half as many will work at their desks, and the rest will sit with Mrs. Watkins learning geometry. How many students will learn geometry?

Ⓐ 2 students

Ⓒ 4 students

Ⓑ 3 students

Ⓓ 6 students

Name

1. The table shows the final score for each friend at the end of a game. Which answer shows the scores listed from least to greatest?

Ⓐ -448.58, -448.65, -450.35, -450.89

Ⓑ -448.65, -448.58, -450.89, -450.35

Ⓒ -450.89, -450.35, -448.65, -448.58

Ⓓ -450.35, -450.89, -448.58, -448.65

Friend	Score
Sandra	-450.35
Russell	-448.65
Amber	-448.58
Sarah	-450.89

2. Mrs. Thompson, the physical-education teacher at Roosevelt Elementary, needs to buy new soccer balls for her gym class. Each soccer ball costs $7.39. For every dozen soccer balls she buys, she gets one ball free. Which expression could be used to find the cost of two dozen soccer balls?

Ⓐ 24 × $7.39

Ⓒ 12 × $7.39

Ⓑ 23 × $7.39

Ⓓ 13 × $7.39

Name _____

1. The table shows how many baskets were made in a free-throw contest. Write each player's statistic as a percentage. Who scored the highest percentage?

Player	Free Throws Made
Heath	$\frac{21}{25} =$
David	$\frac{20}{25} =$
Billy	$\frac{22}{25} =$
Christi	$\frac{19}{25} =$

Answer: _____

2. Rebecca, Melissa, and Linda made a bet about who would score the highest percentage on her multiplication test. The table shows how many questions each girl got correct. What percentage of the questions did each girl get correct on her test?

Friend	Score
Rebecca	47 out of 50 =
Linda	38 out of 50 =
Melissa	41 out of 50 =

Name _____

1. Cody wrote the problem shown below, and Alicia solved it correctly. Which answer did Alicia give? Show your work.

Ⓐ 12   Ⓒ 35

Ⓑ 15   Ⓓ 38

$$6 + 64 \div 2$$

2. A teacher wrote the problem below on the board. The entire class got the answer correct. Which correct answer did the class give? Show your work.

Ⓐ 68   Ⓒ 72

Ⓑ 70   Ⓓ 77

$$(5 + 3)^2 + (5 - 3)^2$$

Name

1. **A.** Use scientific notation to write the number below.

   62,000 = _____

   B. Rewrite the number below in standard form.

   1.85×10^5 = _____

2. Complete the table below by converting the fractions to decimals and percents.

Fraction	Decimal	Percent
$\frac{1}{4}$		
$\frac{1}{2}$		
$\frac{3}{4}$		
$\frac{8}{100}$		
$\frac{3}{5}$		

Name

1. Brandi sells dresses at a store in El Campo, Texas. She earns 7% commission when the store's total sales are under $10,000 and 9% when sales are $10,000 or greater. Last week, the store had $8,200 in sales. This week, the store had $10,803 in sales. How much money did Brandi earn in commission during both weeks combined?

   Answer: _____

2. Chandler wrote the number below and asked Cody to write the number in scientific notation. Write the answer that Cody should have given.

   62,000 ⟶ _____
   Cody's Answer

Name

1. Write the numbers below using scientific notation.

   A. $0.000000824 = $ _____

   B. $7,950,000 = $ _____

   C. $-0.965 = $ _____

2. Write the scientific notations below in standard form.

   A. $2.93 \times 10^7 = $ _____

   B. $6.48 \times 10^{-4} = $ _____

   C. $-3.64 \times 10^{-4} = $ _____

Name

1. Look at the tables below. Complete the tables by converting the given numbers.

A.

Fraction	Percent
$\frac{44}{50}$	

B.

Decimal	Percent
0.4	

C.

Fraction	Percent
$\frac{5}{25}$	

D.

Percent	Decimal
26%	

E.

Percent	Fraction
30%	

F.

Decimal	Percent
0.12	

G.

Decimal	Percent
0.97	

H.

Percent	Decimal
86%	

2. Find the square root of the product in the problem shown below. Show your work.

Ⓐ 44

Ⓑ 12

Ⓒ 64

Ⓓ 24

$$3^2 \times 4^2$$

Name

1. Norma wrote the expression shown in the box on a sheet of paper. James wrote an equation that reflects Norma's expression. Which equation did James write?

Ⓐ $2\frac{3}{4} + 2\frac{1}{2} = 5\frac{1}{4}$

Ⓒ $2\frac{3}{4} - 2\frac{1}{2} = \frac{1}{4}$

Ⓑ $2\frac{1}{2} + 5\frac{1}{4} = 7\frac{3}{4}$

Ⓓ $2\frac{3}{4} \times 2\frac{1}{2} = 6\frac{7}{8}$

> **Norma**
>
> $5\frac{1}{4} - 2\frac{3}{4}$

2. Mark plans to study after school for 30 minutes. He plans to study geometry $\frac{1}{2}$ of the time, problem-solving $\frac{1}{3}$ of the time, and multiplication the rest of the time. How much time will Mark spend studying multiplication?

Answer: _____

Name

1. Jake and Allie are playing a number game. Jake wrote the digits on the cards below to make an 8-digit number. He asked Allie to fill in the missing digit that could make the statement true. If Allie answered correctly, which digit did Allie give?

Ⓐ 9

Ⓑ 2

Ⓒ 4

Ⓓ 1

$$6\ 3\ ,\ 5\ 2\ 3\ ,\ 5\ 1\ \square$$

is
divisible by 4.

2. Kelly scored 54,800,000 points playing a video game. John scored 12,400,000 less points than Kelly. How is the number of points John scored written in scientific notation?

Ⓐ 5.48×10^7

Ⓒ 4.24×10^7

Ⓑ 124×10^5

Ⓓ 124×10^8

Name _____

1. Write the **least common multiple** for each number pair.

A. **10 and 5**

The least common multiple is _____ .

B. **4 and 3**

The least common multiple is _____ .

C. **4 and 12**

The least common multiple is _____ .

2. What sign makes the expression true?

$$5.43 \times 10^4 \bigcirc 5{,}430$$

Ⓐ < Ⓑ > Ⓒ = Ⓓ ≥

Name _____

1. Mrs. Kalinowski gave $\frac{1}{4}$ of her 32 students new calculators. Which expression can be used to find $\frac{1}{4}$ of 32?

Ⓐ $32 \div \frac{1}{4}$ Ⓒ $32 \div 4$

Ⓑ $\frac{1}{4} \div 32$ Ⓓ $32 + 4$

2. David and Christi went camping for the weekend. They took $1\frac{3}{4}$ gallons of water. By the end of the first day, they had used $1\frac{1}{4}$ gallons of water. How much water do David and Christi have left?

Answer: _____

Daily Warm-Up **29**

1. Put the numbers below in order from least to greatest.

0.72	-5.68	$\frac{21}{25}$

————— , ————— , —————

2. Create a factor tree showing the prime factorization for the number 72.

72

Daily Warm-Up **30**

1. Four friends wrote out the factors for $8^4 \times 9^6$. The table shows their answers. Whose answer is correct?

Ⓐ Mike

Ⓑ Matthew

Ⓒ Margo

Ⓓ Mary Beth

Friend	Answer
Mary Beth	$8 \times 8 \times 8 \times 8 \times 9 \times 9 \times 9 \times 9 \times 9 \times 9$
Margo	$8 \times 8 \times 8 \times 9 \times 9 \times 9 \times 9$
Matthew	$8 \times 8 \times 8 \times 8 \times 9 \times 9$
Mike	$8 \times 8 \times 8 \times 9 \times 9 \times 9 \times 9$

2. Heather can type one page in 10 minutes. How many total pages can she type in one hour?

Ⓐ 1 page   Ⓒ 10 pages

Ⓑ 6 pages   Ⓓ 60 pages

Name

1. Four friends wrote lists of common multiples of 4 and 8. The table shows the results. Which friend did this correctly?

Ⓐ Sheri   Ⓒ Nancy

Ⓑ Judy   Ⓓ Stu

Friend	Number
Stu	16, 24, 25, 32, 48
Nancy	16, 24, 40, 48, 56
Judy	16, 20, 28, 32, 48
Sheri	16, 18, 20, 28, 32

2. Which is the correct definition of an integer?

Ⓐ An integer is a whole number.

Ⓑ An integer is a whole number, a negative whole number, or zero.

Ⓒ An integer is a positive number only.

Ⓓ none of the above

Name

1. At a Wharton Junior High Computer Club meeting, 3 out of every 5 students wore a red shirt. 30 students attended the meeting. Which of the following proportions can be used to determine x, the number of students who showed up to the meeting wearing a red shirt?

Ⓐ $\frac{3}{5} = \frac{x}{30}$ Ⓑ $\frac{2}{5} = \frac{30}{x}$ Ⓒ $\frac{2}{5} = \frac{x}{30}$ Ⓓ $\frac{3}{5} = \frac{30}{x}$

2. Students at Red Hill Elementary were asked about their favorite type of music. Based on the table, which fraction shows how many girls like pop music?

Ⓐ $\frac{2}{5}$ Ⓒ $\frac{1}{5}$

Ⓑ $\frac{5}{35}$ Ⓓ $\frac{7}{13}$

Favorite Type of Music

Music	Girls	Boys
Pop	28	24
Country	30	18
Rock	16	10
Jazz	6	8

Name

1. Maddie asked her best friend to loan her $480. Maddie told her friend she would pay 10% interest on the loan. What was the total amount Maddie repaid her friend?

Answer: _____

2. Using the number line below, find the sum of points A, B, and C.

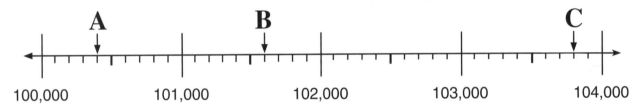

Answer: _____

Name

1. Look at the model below. Which equation represents the model?

   Ⓐ $\sqrt{11} = 121$

   Ⓑ $\sqrt{121} = 11$

   Ⓒ $11 \div 11 = 1$

   Ⓓ $121^2 = 11$

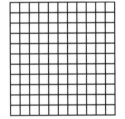

2. On vacation, the Ganske family traveled 75 miles in 1.5 hours of driving. If they drove consistently at the same speed, which proportion could be used to determine how long, h (hours), it will take the Ganske family to travel 325 miles to their grandparents' house?

   Ⓐ $\dfrac{1.5}{325} = \dfrac{75}{h}$

   Ⓑ $\dfrac{325}{1.5} = \dfrac{75}{h}$

   Ⓒ $\dfrac{325}{75} = \dfrac{1.5}{h}$

   Ⓓ $\dfrac{75}{325} = \dfrac{1.5}{h}$

Name

1. Which is *true* about composite numbers?

Ⓐ Composite numbers have only 1 factor.

Ⓑ Composite numbers have only 2 factors.

Ⓒ Composite numbers have 2 or more factors.

Ⓓ Composite numbers are only odd numbers.

2. Which answer shows the **prime factorization** of the number 56?

Ⓐ $2 \times 2 \times 2 \times 2 \times 7$

Ⓑ $2 \times 2 \times 2 \times 7$

Ⓒ $2 \times 2 \times 3 \times 7$

Ⓓ $2 \times 3 \times 7$

Name

1. Which answer best represents the number 7,142,678?

Ⓐ $7 \times 1,000,000 + 2 \times 1,000 + 6 \times 100 + 7 \times 70 + 8 \times 1$

Ⓑ $7 \times 1,000,000 + 1 \times 1,000 + 40 \times 40,000 + 2 \times 1,000 + 6 \times 600 + 78$

Ⓒ $7 \times 1,000,000 + 1 \times 1,000,000 + 4 \times 10,000 + 6 \times 100 + 7 \times 10 + 8 \times 1$

Ⓓ $7 \times 1,000,000 + 1 \times 100,000 + 4 \times 10,000 + 2 \times 1,000 + 6 \times 100 + 7 \times 10 + 8 \times 1$

2. James went to the store to buy pencils for his son. The price for pencils is 3 for $1.50. James paid the clerk $10. What other information is necessary to find James's correct change?

Ⓐ if James used a coupon

Ⓑ how much each pencil costs

Ⓒ how many pencils James bought

Ⓓ if the pencils were on sale

Name

1. Maria wrote one of the fractions below. Jeff wrote the decimal equivalent: 3.08. What improper fraction did Maria write that is equivalent to Jeff's number?

Ⓐ $\frac{56}{25}$

Ⓒ $\frac{19}{5}$

Ⓑ $\frac{77}{25}$

Ⓓ $\frac{32}{5}$

2. Mandy wants to purchase a book that is priced at $20. On Wednesday, they are having a sale for 40% off all the books storewide. How much will Mandy save if she buys the book on Wednesday instead of buying it now?

Answer: _____

Name

1. Write each number in scientific notation.

   A. 760,000 = _____

   C. 5,100,000 = _____

   B. 3,400,000 = _____

   D. 1,400,000 = _____

2. Complete the table below by converting the given decimals into fractions and percents. Fractions must be in simplest form.

Decimal	Fraction	Percent
0.13		
0.5		
0.6		
0.11		
0.82		
0.75		

1. Janice is going on vacation with her husband. Looking at a map, she notices that $\frac{1}{4}$ of an inch represents 4 miles. How many miles would $\frac{3}{4}$ of an inch represent?

Ⓐ 8 miles

Ⓒ 24 miles

Ⓑ 12 miles

Ⓓ 32 miles

2. Mrs. Long took a survey of her 25 students to find their favorite sport. Ten of the 25 students chose tennis, 28% of the students chose basketball, and the remainder of the students chose football. What percentage of students chose tennis, and what percentage chose football? Complete the table.

Tennis	Basketball	Football
	28%	

1. A baseball team won 2 of the 7 games they played. What percentage of the total games played did they lose? Round your answer to the nearest tenth. Explain how you got your answer.

_____

_____

_____

_____

Games Lost = _____%

2. Mr. Chase is the new principal at Davis Junior High. When he was looking at enrollment, he noticed that there are 500 students, 20 English teachers, 10 science teachers, and 20 math teachers at his new school. What is the ratio between the number of math teachers and the number of students at the school? Express your answer as a fraction in lowest terms.

Answer: _____

Name _____

1. Steven wrote the following expression on the board in his classroom. Which answer shows another way to write this expression?

Ⓐ $(7 \times 3) + (5 \times 4)$

Ⓑ $(7 \times 7 \times 7) + (5 \times 5 \times 5 \times 5)$

Ⓒ $(75) + (523)$

Ⓓ $(7 \times 7 \times 7 \times 7) + (5 + 5 + 5 + 5)$

$$7^3 + 5^4$$

2. Mrs. Lee is teaching her students about ratios. To extend the lesson, she wrote the ratio of the number of girls to the number of boys in her class as 3 to 2. There were 18 girls in the class. How many boys are in Mrs. Lee's class?

Answer: _____

Name _____

1. In Friday night's basketball game at Bishop High School, Brandon scored 7 points in the first half and 9 points in the second half of the game. Brandon's total points scored represented $\frac{1}{5}$ of the total points his team scored all together. How many total points did the team score?

Ⓐ 80 points

Ⓒ 45 points

Ⓑ 72 points

Ⓓ 35 points

2. A group of seven students brought enough peppermint candy to share equally among themselves during a computer-lab meeting. Which could be the number of pieces of peppermint candy they brought?

Ⓐ 64

Ⓒ 38

Ⓑ 56

Ⓓ 27

Name

1. Complete the table below by filling in the missing decimals and percentages. Round decimals to the nearest hundredth when necessary.

Fraction	Decimal	Percent
$\frac{1}{2}$		
$\frac{2}{7}$		
$\frac{3}{10}$		
$\frac{4}{5}$		
$\frac{1}{5}$		

2. What does **absolute value** of a number mean?

_____

_____

_____

Can an absolute value be negative? _____

Name

1. What is the absolute value for each of the following numbers?

| **A.** -2 | **B.** 788 | **C.** -144 | **D.** 144 |

_____ _____ _____ _____

2. Simplify the following expressions.

A. -45 + (50 − 5)   **C.** 233 − (-3)

_____   _____

B. -2 + (-1 + 1)   **D.** 3 + (-78)

_____   _____

1. Andrew is buying breakfast for himself and his friend Braydee. Andrew spent $4.50 for 9 donuts. What was the unit price for one donut?

(A) $0.60 per donut

(C) $0.50 per donut

(B) $0.56 per donut

(D) $0.41 per donut

2. Simplify the exponential expressions.

A. $87^2 =$ _____

D. $87^3 =$ _____

B. $99^2 =$ _____

E. $34^3 =$ _____

C. $62^2 =$ _____

F. $17^3 =$ _____

1. At the El Campo Bowling Alley, a tournament is being held to find a champion bowler. The first-place winner will earn a prize of $2,000. The second-place winner will earn 30% less than the first-place winner. The third-place winner will earn 30% less than the second-place winner. Complete the table by writing the correct prize amounts for first, second, and third places.

Place	Prize Amount
First	$
Second	$
Third	$

2. What is 588 trillion written in scientific notation?

(A) 5.88×10^{15}

(C) 5.88×10^{12}

(B) 5.88×10^{14}

(D) 5.88×10^9

Name

1. Linda is driving home from college during Christmas break. Her dorm is 341 miles away from her parents' home. If she drives at an average rate of 62 miles per hour, about how long will it take Linda to get home to see her parents?

Ⓐ 5 hours

Ⓒ 4 hours

Ⓑ $3\frac{1}{4}$ hours

Ⓓ $5\frac{1}{2}$ hours

2. Sandra wrote the following steps on the board. She asked her students to follow the steps to find the mystery number. What is the mystery number?

> Step 1 = Find the product of -8 and -7.
>
> Step 2 = Multiply your answer by 5.
>
> Step 3 = Divide the answer by -5.

Answer: _____

Name

1. A family of 10 went out to dinner to celebrate their grandpa's 86th birthday. Four people ate chicken, half as many people ate meatloaf, and the rest ate steak. How many people ate steak?

Answer: _____

2. Solve the multiplication problems below.

$$7{,}958 \times 730$$

$$9{,}854 \times 573$$

$$8{,}128 \times 403$$

Name

1. Mark is collecting marbles. The ratio of green marbles to red marbles is 36:18. Which of the following ratios is equivalent to 36:18?

Ⓐ 3:1

Ⓒ 18:72

Ⓑ 2:1

Ⓓ 18:24

2. Mrs. Payne asked four students to come to the board and write a number as a fraction, percent, or decimal. The table below shows what they wrote. She then asked the entire class to place the numbers in order from **greatest to least**. Write the answer her students should have given.

Austin	$\frac{2}{3}$
Jaime	72%
Cynthia	$\frac{3}{4}$
Bailey	0.713

_____, _____, _____, _____

Name

1. Robin wrote the number 1,789,634,586. Aliya wrote 1,273,843,299. If Aliya changes the digit in the hundred-millions place to 9, how much greater will her number be than Robin's number?

Answer: _____

2. Which fraction is greater than $\frac{1}{6}$ but less than $\frac{1}{3}$?

Ⓐ $\frac{1}{9}$

Ⓑ $\frac{1}{8}$

Ⓒ $\frac{1}{2}$

Ⓓ $\frac{1}{4}$

1. Look at the number line below. Which letter represents 15 on the number line?

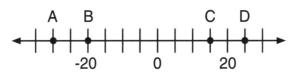

A B   C D

-20   0   20

Ⓐ A   Ⓒ C

Ⓑ B   Ⓓ D

2. Three teachers are going to a conference in Austin, TX. The teachers are traveling together by car at an average rate of 50 miles per hour. If they maintain this speed, how far will they have traveled in $2\frac{1}{2}$ hours?

Answer: _____

1. Margo is baking dessert for her children. The recipe calls for the following 4 ingredients. Put the ingredients in order from **greatest to least** amount needed.

Ingredients	
Flour $1\frac{3}{8}$ cups	Butter 1 cup
Sugar $1\frac{1}{4}$ cups	Milk $1\frac{1}{2}$ cups

_____

_____

_____

_____

2. Look at the integer in the box. Which number is less than the integer?

Ⓐ -897   Ⓒ -9

Ⓑ -63   Ⓓ 0

-654

Name

1. Shade in the number of squares that represent the fraction below. Then write the decimal that is equivalent.

Shade in $\frac{3}{4}$ = 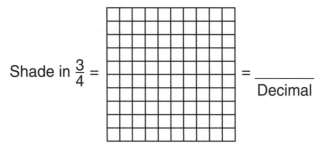 = _____
Decimal

2. Look at the fraction written below. Simplify this fraction and write the decimal equivalent to the fraction.

$$\frac{44}{100} = \frac{\boxed{}}{\boxed{}} = \boxed{}$$

FRACTION **SIMPLIFIED FORM** **DECIMAL**

Name

1. A teacher wrote a range of fractions on the board. She asked her students which range of fractions would the fraction $\frac{3}{5}$ be found in. If the students answered correctly, which group did they choose?

Ⓐ Group 1 Ⓒ Group 3

Ⓑ Group 2 Ⓓ Group 4

Group	Fractions
1	$\frac{4}{10}$ to $\frac{1}{2}$
2	$\frac{5}{10}$ to $\frac{12}{15}$
3	$\frac{12}{15}$ to $\frac{15}{15}$
4	$\frac{1}{3}$ to $\frac{1}{2}$

2. What square root equation does each model represent?

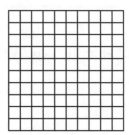

$\sqrt{\rule{2cm}{0.4pt}} = \rule{2cm}{0.4pt}$ $\sqrt{\rule{2cm}{0.4pt}} = \rule{2cm}{0.4pt}$

1. Mrs. Johnsen's savings account pays 3.5% interest each year. What is the decimal equivalent to this percentage?

    Ⓐ   3.5   Ⓒ   0.035

    Ⓑ   0.35   Ⓓ   0.0035

2. At Country Hills Elementary, the principal is checking classes to see what the ratio of girls to boys is in each of the classrooms. The chart shows the number of boys and girls in three classrooms in 2nd grade. Which two classrooms have the same ratio of girls to boys?

Classroom	Wuthrich	Wind	Jackson
Girls	16	20	24
Boys	12	15	16

    Ⓐ   Wuthrich and Wind   Ⓒ   Wind and Jackson

    Ⓑ   Wuthrich and Jackson   Ⓓ   They all have the same ratio of girls to boys.

1. Look at the model below. What decimal does the model represent?

    Ⓐ   4.0   Ⓒ   0.04

    Ⓑ   0.4   Ⓓ   0.0004

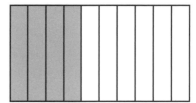

2. Of the 25 students in the drama club, 21 showed up to the after-school meeting. What is the portion of students who showed up to the meeting written as a decimal?

Answer: _____

Name

1. Maci spent 70% of her allowance shopping at the mall. What is 70% written as a decimal?

  Ⓐ 0.07   Ⓒ 0.7

  Ⓑ 1.7   Ⓓ 7.0

2. At Wilson High School, there are 300 students and 40 teachers. What is the student to teacher ratio at Wilson High School? Simplify your answer.

  Ⓐ 3:4   Ⓒ 15:2

  Ⓑ 5:1   Ⓓ 30:1

Name

1. It took Marty 8 hours to drive 420 miles to see his new grandson. What was Marty's average driving speed?

Answer: _____

2. The model below represents $\sqrt{49} = 7$. Add squares to the model to have it represent $\sqrt{81}$.

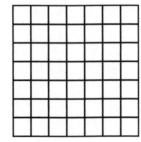

Name

1. Cody wrote the percentage shown in the box. Which value is equivalent to the number Cody wrote?

Ⓐ $\frac{4.82}{100}$

Ⓑ 4.82

Ⓒ 0.482

Ⓓ $\frac{482}{100}$

Cody's Number
48.2%

2. A teacher asked four students to write any number, but to do so only using scientific notation. Which student did this correctly?

Ⓐ	Ⓑ	Ⓒ	Ⓓ
Rory	**Seth**	**Susan**	**Jack**
76,000,000	-45 million	7.5×10^6	75×10^5

Name

1. Jennifer was asked to place the following numbers in order from **least to greatest**. Write the answer Jennifer should have given.

$\frac{2}{3}$	0.17	$\frac{5}{8}$	40%

_____, _____, _____, _____

2. When Jason walked into his class, he saw the following statements written on the board. Which of the following statements is true?

Ⓐ $30\% = \frac{3}{100}$

Ⓑ $60\% = \frac{3}{50}$

Ⓒ $0.30 = \frac{30}{1,000}$

Ⓓ $0.06 = \frac{3}{50}$

1. Gina wrote the scientific notation value below. Which answer shows the number Gina wrote in **standard form**?

> **Gina's Problem**
>
> 1.5×10^{-3}

Ⓐ 1,500   Ⓑ 3.15   Ⓒ 0.00015   Ⓓ 0.0015

2. Four friends wrote the fractions below. Who wrote the fraction with the least value?

Ⓐ Amber   Ⓒ Sarah

Ⓑ Libby   Ⓓ Brenda

Friend	Fraction
Amber	$\frac{3}{4}$
Libby	$\frac{2}{3}$
Sarah	$\frac{5}{6}$
Brenda	$\frac{7}{12}$

1. Mary wrote the statements below. Which of Mary's statements is true?

Ⓐ $\frac{3}{5} > \frac{5}{9}$ Ⓒ $\frac{3}{5} = \frac{5}{9}$

Ⓑ $\frac{5}{9} - \frac{3}{4} = \frac{1}{2}$ Ⓓ $\frac{3}{5} < \frac{5}{9}$

2. Which statement below is a true statement?

Ⓐ -5 < -6   Ⓒ -7 > 2

Ⓑ -6 > -5   Ⓓ -7 < -6

Warm-Up 1
1. 55 miles per hour
2. 1.5 pints of paint

Warm-Up 2
1. $2.10 per foot   2. 88%

Warm-Up 3
1. 36
2. 42 gallons of gas in 14 days

Warm-Up 4
1. $\frac{7}{20}$ 2. $\frac{1}{4}$; 0.237

Warm-Up 5
1. $\frac{3}{4}$, 72%, 0.713, $\frac{2}{3}$
2. Richard, Brenda, Sarah, Teresa

Warm-Up 6
1. C   2. **A.** 6
         B. 12

Warm-Up 7
1. **A.** 5   **C.** 21
   B. 4   **D.** 8
2. **A.** 39,000   **C.** 98,000,000
   B. 0.000067

Warm-Up 8
1. <   2. B

Warm-Up 9
1. B   2. D

Warm-Up 10
1. **A.** $\sqrt{36} = 6$ **B.** $\sqrt{81} = 9$

2.
Fraction	Decimal	Percent
$\frac{1}{2}$	0.5	**50%**
$\frac{1}{4}$	**0.25**	25%
$\frac{1}{5}$	0.2	20%
$\frac{2}{5}$	0.4	**40%**

Warm-Up 11
1. C   2. $\frac{12}{25}$, $2\frac{1}{4}$

Warm-Up 12
1. 0.24   2. Red

Warm-Up 13
1. $287   2. C

Warm-Up 14
1. A
2. $12.99 × 0.25
   $9.74

Warm-Up 15
1. D   2. B

Warm-Up 16
1. C   2. C

Warm-Up 17
1. C   2. C

Warm-Up 18
1. C   2. B

Warm-Up 19
1. Heath = 84%
   David = 80%
   Billy = 88%
   Christi = 76%
   Highest percentage = Billy
2. Rebecca 94%, Linda 76%, Melissa 82%

Warm-Up 20
1. D   2. A

Warm-Up 21
1. **A.** $6.2 × 10^4$ **B.** 185,000
2.
Fraction	Decimal	Percent
$\frac{1}{4}$	0.25	25%
$\frac{1}{2}$	0.50	50%
$\frac{3}{4}$	0.75	75%
$\frac{8}{100}$	0.08	8%
$\frac{3}{5}$	0.6	60%

Warm-Up 22
1. $1,546.27   2. $6.2 × 10^4$

Warm-Up 23
1. **A.** $8.24 × 10^{-7}$ 2. **A.** 29,300,000
   B. $7.95 × 10^6$ **B.** 0.000648
   C. $-9.65 × 10^{-1}$ **C.** -0.000364

Warm-Up 24
1. **A.** 88%   **E.** $\frac{3}{10}$ or $\frac{30}{100}$
   B. 40%   **F.** 12%
   C. 20%   **G.** 97%
   D. 0.26   **H.** 0.86
2. B

Warm-Up 25
1. A   2. 5 minutes

Warm-Up 26
1. B   2. C

Warm-Up 27
1. **A.** 10   2. B
   B. 12
   C. 12

Warm-Up 28
1. C   2. $\frac{1}{2}$ gallon

Warm-Up 29
1. -5.68, 0.72, $\frac{21}{25}$
2. Possible answer:

Warm-Up 30
1. D   2. B

Warm-Up 31
1. C   2. B

Warm-Up 32
1. A   2. C

Warm-Up 33
1. $528   2. 305,800

Warm-Up 34
1. B   2. D

Warm-Up 35
1. C   2. B

Warm-Up 36
1. D   2. C

Warm-Up 37
1. B   2. $8

Warm-Up 38

1. **A.** 7.6×10^5 **C.** 5.1×10^6
   B. 3.4×10^6 **D.** 1.4×10^6

2.

Decimal	Fraction	Percent
0.13	$\frac{13}{100}$	13%
0.5	$\frac{1}{2}$	50%
0.6	$\frac{3}{5}$	60%
0.11	$\frac{11}{100}$	11%
0.82	$\frac{41}{50}$	82%
0.75	$\frac{3}{4}$	75%

Warm-Up 39

1. B

2. Tennis: 40%
   Football: 32%

Warm-Up 40

1. 71.4%
   Divide the # of games won (5) by the total number of games (7). Convert the decimal into a percentage.

2. $\frac{1}{25}$

Warm-Up 41

1. B   2. 12

Warm-Up 42

1. A   2. B

Warm-Up 43

1.

Fraction	Decimal	Percent
$\frac{1}{2}$	0.5	50%
$\frac{2}{7}$	0.29	29%
$\frac{3}{10}$	0.3	30%
$\frac{4}{5}$	0.8	80%
$\frac{1}{5}$	0.2	20%

2. the non-negative volume of a number (how far that number is from zero); no

Warm-Up 44

1. **A.** 2   **C.** 144
   B. 788   **D.** 144

2. **A.** 0   **C.** 236
   B. -2   **D.** -75

Warm-Up 45

1. C

2. **A.** 7,569   **D.** 658,503
   B. 9,801   **E.** 39,304
   C. 3,844   **F.** 4,913

Warm-Up 46

1. 1st: $2,000   2. B
   2nd: $1,400
   3rd: $980

Warm-Up 47

1. D   2. -56

Warm-Up 48

1. 4 people   2. 5,809,340
                  5,646,342
                  3,275,584

Warm-Up 49

1. B

2. $\frac{3}{4}$, 72%, 0.713, $\frac{2}{3}$

Warm-Up 50

1. 184,208,713   2. D

Warm-Up 51

1. C   2. 125 miles

Warm-Up 52

1. Milk, Flour, Sugar, Butter

2. A

Warm-Up 53

1. 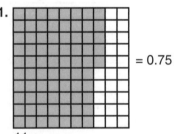   = 0.75

2. $\frac{11}{25}$ = 0.44

Warm-Up 54

1. B   2. $\sqrt{49} = 7$
           $\sqrt{100} = 10$

Warm-Up 55

1. C   2. A

Warm-Up 56

1. B   2. 0.84

Warm-Up 57

1. C   2. C

Warm-Up 58

1. 52.5 MPH

2.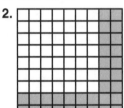

Warm-Up 59

1. C   2. C

Warm-Up 60

1. 0.17, 40%, $\frac{5}{8}$, $\frac{2}{3}$

2. D

Warm-Up 61

1. D   2. D

Warm-Up 62

1. A   2. D

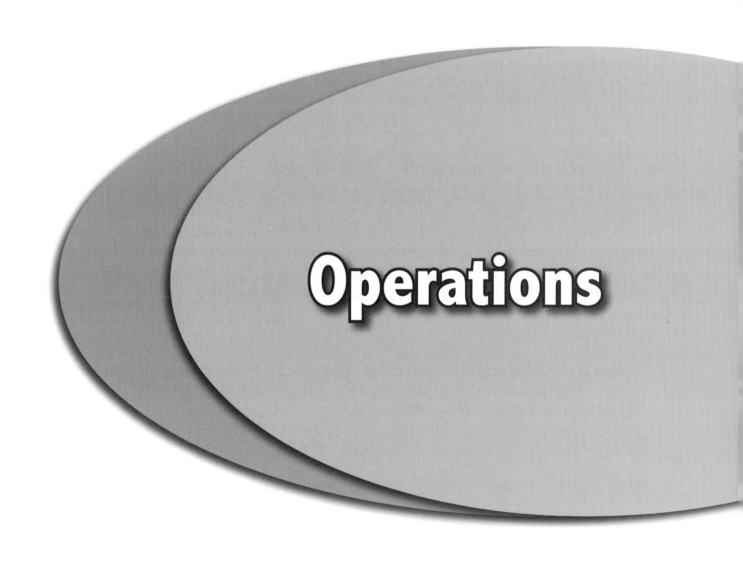

Operations

Name

1. Armando spent $8.76 on 6 bags of chips. How much did each bag of chips cost?

Ⓐ $1.26

Ⓒ $1.56

Ⓑ $1.46

Ⓓ $1.76

2. Connie earned $204 working a catering job on Saturday for Junior's Steak House. She worked 8 hours. How much did Connie earn each hour?

Answer: _____

Name

1. Michael is making a map of his school. He used a scale in which 2 inches represents 15 feet. What proportion would correctly show a way to determine the number of feet represented by 3 inches on the map?

Ⓐ $\frac{15}{3} = \frac{x}{2}$

Ⓒ $\frac{15}{2} = \frac{x}{3}$

Ⓑ $\frac{2}{3} = \frac{x}{15}$

Ⓓ $\frac{2}{x} = \frac{15}{3}$

2. Marvin owns 120 rare baseball cards. 40 of the cards are worth $200 each, 60 are worth $150 each, and the rest of the cards are worth $75 each. Which number sentence can be used to find how much money Marvin will make if he sells all 120 baseball cards?

Ⓐ (40 × $200) + (60 × $150) + (40 × $75) = _____

Ⓑ (40 × $150) + (60 × $200) + (20 × $75) = _____

Ⓒ (40 × $100) + (60 × $200) + (20 × $75) = _____

Ⓓ (40 × $200) + (60 × $150) + (20 × $75) = _____

1. The model below represents $3x + 1 = 7$. What is the last step in finding the value of x?

| X | X | X | + ▲ = ▲ ▲ ▲ ▲ ▲ ▲ ▲

Ⓐ Divide 6 into 3 equal groups.

Ⓑ Subtract 1 counter from each side.

Ⓒ Add 1 counter to each side.

Ⓓ Subtract 1 from 7.

2. Jackie wrote the problem below on the board. What is the value of the expression Jackie wrote?

$$7 + -3$$

Answer: _____

1. Lydia wrote the problem and answer shown below on the board. Which answer choice shows how Doris could check Lydia's answer.

Lydia's Problem

12.9 divided by 8.6
is equal to 1.5

Ⓐ multiply 1.5 by 8.6   Ⓒ multiply 12.9 by 12.9

Ⓑ multiply 1.5 by 12.9   Ⓓ multiply 12.9 by 8.6

2. Wayne wants to barbeque a brisket for his family. At a meat market, Wayne can buy a full brisket or half a brisket. The brisket Wayne is looking at weighs about 8.3 pounds. If Wayne decides to buy half the brisket, which expression can be used to find the weight of the brisket that Wayne will purchase?

Ⓐ 8.3 multiplied by 0.5   Ⓒ 8.3 divided by 0.5

Ⓑ 0.5 divided by 8.3   Ⓓ 0.5 plus 8.3

1. Mandy sells computers for a company called Computer World. She earns 5% commission on her sales. Her commission last month was $700. What was Mandy's total sales for that month?

Ⓐ $140

Ⓑ $700

Ⓒ $705

Ⓓ $14,000

2. Jax is buying a Father's Day gift for his dad. He buys a pair of running shoes that cost $140. If Jax uses a coupon for 20% off, what is the cost of the running shoes before tax?

Answer: _____

1. Solve for *m*.

$$\frac{32}{40} = \frac{m}{30}$$

m = _____

2. Each week, Gordon has a goal to put 20% of his paycheck in the bank. This week, Gordon's paycheck is $125.52. How much will Gordon need to put into his savings account to meet his goal?

$ _____ →

SAVINGS

1. Margo forgot how to simplify an expression. Which part of the expression should she simplify first?

(A) $6 + 3$

(B) 3^3

(C) $3 \cdot 2$

(D) $2 \div 3$

> **Margo's Problem**
>
> $6 + 3 \cdot 2 \div 3^3 - 10$

2. Look at the problem below. What should be the first step in solving the problem?

(A) multiply 4×3

(B) divide 6 by 2

(C) calculate exponents

(D) multiply 4×3, then add 6

> $4 \times 3^2 + 6 \div 2$

1. A teacher wrote the expression below on the board. Four student groups worked on the problem to find the answer. The table shows their answers. Which group answered correctly?

Teacher's Problem	Group 1	Group 2	Group 3	Group 4
$40 \div 4 \times (3 - 1)$	8	5	20	29

(A) Group 4   (B) Group 3   (C) Group 2   (D) Group 1

2. The cost of each ticket for a one-act play at Roosevelt High School is $4. Which of the following expressions represents the price of t tickets to the play?

(A) $4 \div t$

(B) $4 \cdot t$

(C) $3 - t$

(D) $3 + t$

1. Twin sisters are in the same math class at Wharton Junior High. Tanya spent 9 hours studying for a geometry test. Her sister, Tammy, spent $\frac{3}{8}$ of that time studying for the same test. How many more hours did Tanya study than Tammy.

Ⓐ $3\frac{2}{8}$ hours

Ⓒ $4\frac{3}{8}$ hours

Ⓑ $5\frac{5}{8}$ hours

Ⓓ $5\frac{3}{8}$ hours

2. Doris paid $1.16 for 2 pounds of lemons. Sheri bought 3 pounds of lemons for the same price per pound as Doris paid. What was the total amount that Sheri paid for the lemons?

Answer: _____

1. 226 family members will be attending Sandy's great-great-grandmother's 100th birthday. Sandy, her husband, her 9 children, and the guest of honor will sit at the head table. All other tables will seat 8 guests. Which expression will help determine how many more tables Sandy will need?

Ⓐ $(226 - 12) \div 8$

Ⓒ $226 \div 8 - 12$

Ⓑ $226 \div 8 + 12$

Ⓓ $(226 \div 12) \div 8$

2. At Sam's Sporting Goods, the owner cut 15% of the budget for each of the 4 departments in the store. What fraction of the store's total budget is being cut? Simplify your answer.

Answer: _____

Name

1. Which answer choice shows decimals in order from greatest to least?

   Ⓐ 0.13   0.5   0.07

   Ⓑ 0.07   0.13   0.5

   Ⓒ 0.5   0.13   0.07

   Ⓓ 0.13   0.07   0.5

2. Solve the problem: $12 \times (-5)$.

   Ⓐ 60   Ⓒ -60

   Ⓑ -17   Ⓓ 50

Name

1. Beverly works from home as a blogger. During a 3-month period, Beverly replied to more than 36 postings every day, 7 days a week. Which answer could **not** be the total number of responses Beverly posted for the given period?

   Ⓐ 3,200   Ⓒ 4,200

   Ⓑ 3,245   Ⓓ 3,545

2. Sarah and Denae work at Sports City. Last week, Sarah worked 122 hours, which is more than twice the number of hours Denae (d) worked during the same week. Which inequality represents the number of hours worked by both girls?

   Ⓐ $122 > d - 2$ Ⓒ $122 < 2 + d$

   Ⓑ $122 > 2d$ Ⓓ $122 < 2d$

1. Larry went grocery shopping for his son's birthday party. He decided to grill hot dogs for his guests. Each package had 10 hot dogs. Each package of hot-dog buns had 8 buns. Larry purchased 9 packages of hot dogs and 11 packages of hot-dog buns. Write an expression that shows how many more hot dogs than hot dog buns Larry purchased.

Answer: _____

2. Marco uses 2 gallons of gas to drive 42 miles in his truck. How many miles can Marco drive if he plans on using 6 gallons of gas?

Answer: _____

1. Wanda's children love to eat cereal for breakfast. Every day, her family eats about $\frac{2}{3}$ of a cereal box. At this rate, how many boxes of cereal will Wanda need to buy to have enough cereal to feed her kids breakfast for 1 week?

Answer: _____

2. Two customers were standing in line to purchase deli meat. James bought 2 pounds of salami for $7.50. Hank bought $5\frac{1}{2}$ pounds of salami. How much did Hank spend on salami?

Answer: _____

1. Peggy is p years old. Jim's age, j, is 3 more than 4 times Peggy's age. Which of the following equations best represents their ages?

Ⓐ $p = (3 + 4)j$

Ⓒ $j = 4p + 3$

Ⓑ $p = 4j + 3$

Ⓓ $j = (4 + 3)p$

2. Amber works at a zoo. One of her jobs is to feed the exotic birds. Each morning, she starts off her day with $7\frac{9}{10}$ buckets of seed. Today, after spending the morning feeding the birds, she now has $3\frac{1}{10}$ buckets left. How many buckets of seed did Amber use that morning?

Ⓐ $2\frac{3}{5}$ buckets

Ⓑ $3\frac{3}{5}$ buckets

Ⓒ $4\frac{4}{5}$ buckets

Ⓓ $5\frac{5}{5}$ buckets

1. Briana is buying jeans for her daughter. The retail price for the jeans is $40. She has a coupon for 20% off. If the tax on the jeans is 8% of the reduced price, what will Briana pay for the jeans?

Answer: _____

2. At her birthday party, Janice and her guests ate $\frac{1}{5}$ of a chocolate cake. That night, she left and went to the movies with friends. When she arrived home, only $\frac{3}{10}$ of the cake was left. What fraction describes the amount of cake that was eaten while Janice was at the movies with her friends? Simplify your answer.

Answer: _____

Name

1. Look at the display on the calculator. If the number on the display is the divisor, and 946 is the quotient, what is the dividend?

Answer: _____

2. Robert earns $95 for 3 hours of work. At that rate, how long would he have to work to earn $200?

Answer: _____

Name

1. Sarah is the new office manager at a local bank. She earns $36 for working 3 hours. At that rate, about how long would Sarah need to work to earn $720?

Answer: _____

2. Four students wrote math problems along with the answers. The table shows their work. Which friend answered his or her problem correctly?

Ⓐ Liz

Ⓑ Jessica

Ⓒ Jay Paul

Ⓓ Troy

Student	Problem	Answer
Jessica	(+6) × (-2)	-12
Troy	(+5) × (+7)	+2
Jay Paul	(-7) × (-5)	-35
Liz	(-9) × (-7)	-63

Name

1. Use comparative symbols to compare the fractions below.

A. $\frac{31}{12}$ ◯ $\frac{15}{4}$

B. $\frac{11}{7}$ ◯ $\frac{15}{9}$

C. $\frac{20}{8}$ ◯ $\frac{3}{11}$

D. $\frac{1}{8}$ ◯ $\frac{21}{2}$

2. David wrote one true statement and 3 false statements. Which statement below is the **true** statement that David wrote?

Ⓐ $\frac{5}{9} - \frac{3}{5} = \frac{1}{2}$

Ⓑ $\frac{3}{5} = \frac{5}{9}$

Ⓒ $\frac{3}{5} > \frac{5}{9}$

Ⓓ $\frac{3}{5} < \frac{5}{9}$

Name

1. Misty and Mandy are twin sisters. They're both studying for a math test. Misty studied $\frac{1}{4}$ of an hour and Mandy studied $\frac{3}{4}$ of an hour. How many more minutes did Mandy study than Misty?

Answer: _____

2. Simplify the expression in the box. Which answer choice is the correct answer?

Ⓐ 20

Ⓑ 28

Ⓒ 54

Ⓓ 59

$$43 \times (3^2 - 2^3) + (5^1 - 1^5)^2$$

1. Which would be the best way to solve the equation below?

Ⓐ Add 6 to both sides to find the value of *y*.

Ⓑ Subtract 6 from both sides to find the value of *y*.

Ⓒ Multiply both sides by 6 to find the value of *y*.

Ⓓ Divide both sides by 6 to find the value of *y*.

> **Equation**
>
> $6y = 54$

2. Four students wrote the problems below. Which problem was simplified correctly?

Ⓐ $2^5 - (13 - 5) + 4^2 - 2 \times 3 = 54$

Ⓑ $2^5 - (13 - 5) + 4^2 - 2 \times 3 = 4$

Ⓒ $2^5 - (13 - 5) + 4^2 - 2 \times 3 = 22$

Ⓓ $2^5 - (13 - 5) + 4^2 - 2 \times 3 = 34$

1. Look at the problem below. Which is the first step in simplifying this type of problem?

$$12 \div 4 + (2^4 \times (9 - 6) + 3^2 + 4)$$

Ⓐ Add from left to right.

Ⓑ Multiply from left to right.

Ⓒ Solve inside the parentheses.

Ⓓ Divide from left to right.

2. Alyssa worked out one of the expressions in the table and came up with 3 as the answer. Which problem did she simplify?

Ⓐ problem 1

Ⓑ problem 2

Ⓒ problem 3

Ⓓ problem 4

Problem	Expression
1	$6^2 \div 4 \times (3 - 1)$
2	$7^4 \div 7 \times (5 - 1)$
3	$3^4 \div 9 \times (6 - 3)$
4	$4^4 \div 8 \times (6 - 4)$

1. In Mrs. Johnsen's class, she has a total of 52 books for her reading groups. She handed out an equal number of books to each of her four reading groups. She reserved 24 books to hand out at a later time. How many books did each reading group get?

Answer: _____

2. Susan wrote the problem below. What value goes in the box to make the equation true?

Ⓐ $\frac{1}{2}$ Ⓒ $\frac{5}{3}$

Ⓑ $\frac{3}{2}$ Ⓓ $\frac{2}{3}$

$$\boxed{} = \frac{12}{10} \div \frac{4}{5}$$

1. Dorothy is buying 2 pounds of deli meat for $6.50. Which expression could be used to represent the cost of 3.5 pounds of deli meat?

Ⓐ $3.5 + 2(\$6.50)$

Ⓑ $3.5\left(\dfrac{2}{\$6.50}\right)$

Ⓒ $\$6.50 \div \dfrac{3.5}{2}$

Ⓓ $\$6.50 \div 2(3.50)$

2. Jack is called to the board by his teacher to simplify the expression shown below. Which of the following should be performed first?

Ⓐ $2 \div 3$ Ⓒ $3 \cdot 2$

Ⓑ $5 + 3$ Ⓓ 3^3

$$5 + 3 \cdot 2 \div 3^3 - 12$$

1. Examine the expression in the box. What is the value of the expression when $x = 1$ and $y = 4$? Show your work.

   Ⓐ 17

   Ⓑ 21

   Ⓒ 69

   Ⓓ 70

   $$5x + y^3$$

2. Becky plans to spend a total of 30 minutes doing chores before heading to the movies with her children. She plans to make the beds, clean the restroom, and wash dishes. She made the beds for $\frac{1}{3}$ of the total time, washed the dishes for $\frac{1}{2}$ of the total time, and cleaned the bathroom the remainder of the time. How much time did it take for her to clean the bathroom?

   Answer: _____

1. Mrs. Peña, a 3rd-grade math teacher, is buying 27 notebooks for her students. Each notebook costs $5.89. Because Mrs. Peña is a teacher, she will receive a 10% discount on items purchased for her classroom. How much will Mrs. Peña pay for the 27 notebooks before tax?

   Answer: _____

2. Amber, Cody, and Russell entered a contest and won $2,000. Cody gets $\frac{1}{2}$ of the money. Russell gets $\frac{3}{4}$ of the remaining money. What fraction of the winnings and what amount of money will Amber receive?

   Ⓐ $\frac{1}{2}$ of the money, which is $500

   Ⓑ $\frac{3}{4}$ of the money, which is $750

   Ⓒ $\frac{1}{8}$ of the money, which is $250

   Ⓓ $\frac{1}{4}$ of the money, which is $150

1. Brent spent $54 buying 12 gallons of gas. How much money did Brent pay per gallon?

Answer: _____

2. A store manager ordered chips for his store. A bag of chips costs $1.49. There are 36 bags of chips in each box. If the store manager orders more than $200 worth of product, the store will receive a 10% discount on the cost of the order. The store manager orders 12 boxes of chips. What is the total cost of the chip order using the 10% discount, if it applies?

Answer: _____

1. Michael's soccer team won 12 out of the 16 games they played. Write the amount of games won as a percentage and as a simplified fraction.

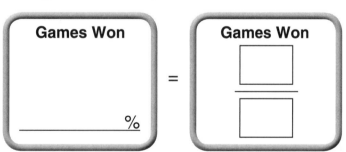

2. Last year, Yolanda earned $6 an hour babysitting for her neighbor's two young children. This year, she is earning $8 an hour babysitting. How much was Yolanda's raise to the nearest whole percent?

Answer: _____

Name

1. Simplify the expression below following the order of operations. Show your work for each step of the process.

$$32 + (8 \div 2) \bullet 3 - 1 + 3^3$$

Answer: _____

2. In Mr. Roddy's 7th-grade math class, 15 of the 25 students live within 10 miles of school. Which value does not represent the part of the class that lives within a 10-mile radius of school?

Ⓐ $\frac{10}{15}$ Ⓑ $\frac{3}{5}$ Ⓒ 0.6 Ⓓ 60%

Name

1. Rebecca needs gas for her small car. She spent $34.00 for 12 gallons of gas. If her husband fills up his truck at the same place and pays the same price per gallon, how many gallons could he buy for $51.00?

Ⓐ 15 gallons Ⓑ 16 gallons Ⓒ 17 gallons Ⓓ 18 gallons

2. EJ, James, Tyler, and Elia took a math test. The table shows the number of problems each of them missed. Write the percentage of correct answers in order from greatest to least along with the students' names. Make sure you round your answers to the nearest hundredth.

Name	Number Missed
Elia	10 out of 45
James	12 out of 45
EJ	20 out of 45
Tyler	16 out of 45

% Correct (Greatest to Least)

_____ _____%

_____ _____%

_____ _____%

_____ _____%

Name

1. A teacher in Wharton, Texas, works 10 months out of a year. What percent of the year does this teacher work? (Round your answer to the nearest hundredth.)

Answer: _____

2. Use prime factorization to complete the factor trees. Be sure to show your work.

A. 99

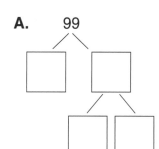

B. 36

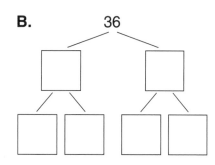

C. 54

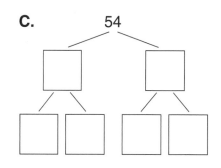

Name

1. Compare the fractions using the correct symbols.

A. $\dfrac{14}{7}$ ◯ $\dfrac{4}{6}$

B. $\dfrac{1}{3}$ ◯ $\dfrac{1}{2}$

C. $\dfrac{6}{11}$ ◯ $\dfrac{25}{5}$

2. Latoya worked on the math problems below. Which problem has 35 as the answer?

Ⓐ Problem A

Ⓑ Problem B

Ⓒ Problem C

Ⓓ Problem D

Problems	
Problem A	(+6) × (-2) = _____
Problem B	(+7) × (-5) = _____
Problem C	(-7) × (-5) = _____
Problem D	(-8) × (-2) = _____

1. Michael spends $10 a month washing his truck. How much will it cost for Michael to wash his truck during a 5-year span?

Answer: _____

2. Solve the following problems.

A. 785	**B.** 785	**C.** 785	**D.** 785
$\times$ 79	$\times$ 39	$\times$ 69	$\times$ 89

1. Mondo went shopping for new tools. He bought a drill for $179.83, a new electric saw for $124.58, and a new air compressor for $245.43. Mondo had a coupon for a 10% discount off the air compressor. How much did Mondo spend on all 3 items before tax?

Answer: _____

2. At a store in Wharon, 2 pieces of candy cost 15 cents. How much will 2 dozen pieces of candy cost?

Answer: _____

1. Kendall is saving money for 3 new video games. So far, he has $100 saved in his piggy bank. Each week, he plans to add $8 to his piggy bank. Which equation below can be used to determine the number of weeks (*w*) it will take Kendall to earn the $220 necessary to buy the 3 video games?

   Ⓐ $8w + 100 = 220$

   Ⓑ $8w - 100 = 220$

   Ⓒ $220 + 100 = 8w$

   Ⓓ $8 + w = 220$

2. Brandi went clothes shopping for college. She bought 4 new shirts and 6 pairs of jeans. The 4 shirts cost $55 each, and the 6 pairs of jeans cost $95 each. Which equation can be used to find the total cost of the 4 shirts and 6 pairs of jeans?

   Ⓐ $p = (4 \times 55) + (6 \times 95)$

   Ⓑ $p = (4 \times 6) + (55 \times 95)$

   Ⓒ $p = (4 \times 6) + (55 \times 4)$

   Ⓓ $p = (4 \times 95) + (6 \times 55)$

1. Lourdes had 5.6 gigabytes of pictures of her grandchildren stored on a flash drive. She deleted 40% of the pictures to make room for new ones. How many gigabytes of photos did she delete?

   Answer: _____

2. In a 7th-grade math class, the students are learning about greatest common factors. The teacher wrote the numbers 63, 42, and 105 on the board and asked her students to find the greatest common factor for these numbers. What correct answer did the class give?

   Answer: _____

1. Look at the equations in the table. Which value can be substituted for x to make all the equations true?

   Ⓐ 4

   Ⓑ 6

   Ⓒ 8

   Ⓓ 12

$6x - 9 = 39$	$5x - 9 = 31$
$3x - 12 = 12$	$9x - 4 = 68$

2. Four students went to a CD wholesale store to buy old music CDs. Together, they spent $20 on 1 music CD from the 1970s and 4 CDs from the 1980s. The CD from the 1970s cost $12. Which equation can be used to find c, the cost of each CD from the 1980s?

   Ⓐ $20 = 4c + 12$

   Ⓑ $20 = 12c + 4$

   Ⓒ $20c = 12 + 4$

   Ⓓ $20 = c + 4 + 12$

1. Robin is throwing a party for a charity. She and her friends have sold 549 tickets. 431 of the tickets are adult tickets, which sell for $12 each, and the remaining tickets are child tickets that sell for $8 each. How much total money has Robin raised for her charity?

   Answer: _____

2. Rita's Snow Cone Stand is open five months of the year. The table below shows expenses and sales during a three-month time frame. What was the profit or loss for Rita's Snow Cone Stand for June through August?

Month	Sales	Expenses
June	$842	$1,200
July	$1,800	$75
August	$1,350	$320
Totals		

   Profit/Loss

   $ _____

1. Which statement about the **commutative property of addition** is true?

Ⓐ The order in which the numbers in an expression are combined affects the value of that expression.

Ⓑ The order in which the numbers in an expression are placed affects the value of that expression.

Ⓒ The order in which the numbers in an expression are placed does not affect the value of that expression.

Ⓓ Grouping affects the value of the expression.

2. Use the distributive property to simplify the expression. Be sure to simplify completely.

$$3(4x + 6) + 7x =$$

---

1. Use the distributive property to simplify the expression. Be sure to simplify completely.

$$7(9x + 3) + 2x =$$

2. Which answer choice below is *not* correct?

Ⓐ $\sqrt{100} = 10$ since $10^2 = 100$

Ⓑ $\sqrt{144} = 12$ since $12^2 = 144$

Ⓒ $\sqrt{121} = 11$ since $11^2 = 22$

Ⓓ $\sqrt{64} = 8$ since $8^2 = 64$

Name

1. What would be the first step in simplifying the expression shown in the box? Now simplify the expression.

Ⓐ Multiply and divide from left to right.

Ⓑ Simplify all exponents.

Ⓒ Add and subtract from left to right.

Ⓓ Do operations in parentheses.

$$18 \div (8 - 2) + 2^2 \bullet 7 - 11$$

2. Look at the problem in the box. Which is the correct first step in simplifying the expression? Be sure to simplify completely.

Ⓐ $8 - 3$

Ⓑ 3^2

Ⓒ $5 + 2^3$

Ⓓ 2×7

$$(8 - 3)^2 \div 5 + 2^3 \times 7$$

Name

1. Sarah has completed $\frac{5}{8}$ of her job responsibilities. What percentage of Sarah's job responsibilities has she already completed?

Ⓐ 62.5%

Ⓑ 16%

Ⓒ 6.50%

Ⓓ 1.60%

2. Patricia spent $\frac{3}{8}$ of her time cleaning her room. She spent $\frac{2}{5}$ as much time washing dishes as she did cleaning her room. What fraction of time did Patricia spend washing dishes? Simplify your answer.

Answer: _____

Name

1. Doris's computer crashed. She has rebuilt 40% of the computer using new parts. What fraction of her computer is still the old parts?

(A) $\frac{4}{5}$ (B) $\frac{6}{100}$ (C) $\frac{3}{5}$ (D) $\frac{1}{40}$

2. Melissa is playing a video game. She made it to the second level of the game in 30 minutes. At the same rate, how long will it take Melissa to make it to the 5th level of the game?

(A) 160 minutes   (C) 35 minutes

(B) 75 minutes   (D) 60 minutes

Name

1. Of the first 15 marbles Chandler pulled from a bag, 9 of the marbles were solid red. At the same rate, how many marbles would have to be pulled out of the bag for 90 of them to be solid red?

Answer: _____

2. Out of the 81 students in the Wharton Band, 54 won ribbons at the last contest. What is the ratio of students who won ribbons to the total number of students in the band?

(A) 2:1   (B) 2:3   (C) 1:27   (D) 7:27

1. Cody is on the baseball team at school. He can hit the ball 65% of the time. If he tries hitting the ball 30 times in a row, how many balls will he hit? Round to the nearest whole number.

Answer: _____

2. Terry has a bag of candy she can share equally among either 3, 5, or 6 students in her class without any being left over. What is the least amount of candy that can be in the bag?

Ⓐ 3 pieces   Ⓑ 15 pieces   Ⓒ 20 pieces   Ⓓ 30 pieces

1. Jenny collects buttons. She has divided 800 buttons into 3 separate jars. She has 170 in the first jar and 150 more in the second jar than she has in the third jar. How many buttons does Jenny have in the second jar?

Answer: _____

2. Larry went to the beach with his son. He collected seashells and placed them into three piles. He placed 183 seashells in the first pile. He placed 109 less seashells in the second pile than in the first pile. The third pile has exactly the sum of piles one and two. How many seashells were in the third pile?

Answer: _____

Name

1. Sheri is looking for Christmas gifts for her daughters. She purchased a necklace that was originally $24 for her oldest daughter. The necklace was on sale for 20% off. How much did Sheri pay before tax?

Answer: _____

2. What is the first step in evaluating the expression shown below? Simplify the expression.

Ⓐ parentheses

Ⓑ exponents

Ⓒ division

Ⓓ multiplication

$$24 \div 6 + 2^4 \times (9 - 6) + (3^2 + 4)$$

Name

1. Linda loves watching for birds on Saturday walks. Of the birds she saw this past Saturday, she saw only mockingbirds and blue jays. $\frac{2}{5}$ of the birds she saw were mockingbirds. What was the ratio of mockingbirds to blue jays Linda saw on her walk?

Ⓐ 5:2

Ⓒ 2:5

Ⓑ 3:2

Ⓓ 2:3

2. Marco, Tony, Hannah, and Jennifer solved the math problem shown below. The table shows their answers. Which person answered correctly?

$$4^2 \times (3^2 - 2^3) + (5^1 - 5)^2$$

Jennifer	Tony	Hannah	Marco
100	96	16	80

Ⓐ Marco   Ⓑ Hannah   Ⓒ Tony   Ⓓ Jennifer

Name

1. Write a short definition for each of the following terms. Give an example for each.

Distributive Property _____

_____

Example: _____

Commutative Property _____

_____

Example: _____

2. Chloe has a picture of her cat. She wants to reduce the picture on a copier machine. The picture is 12 inches tall and 18 inches wide. If she reduces the width by 3 inches, how tall will the picture be?

Answer: _____

Name

1. Sandra is driving 546 miles to her grandmother's home for Thanksgiving. In 4 hours, she drove 312 miles. How long will it take Sandra to drive the rest of the way if she drives at the same speed?

Ⓐ 3.5 hours   Ⓒ 2.5 hours

Ⓑ 3 hours   Ⓓ 2 hours

2. Solve the two problems below. Show your work.

   A. Find 75% of 200.

   B. Find 30% of 150.

Name

1. Marsha wants to buy a new microwave. The microwave is on sale for 75% off the regular price of $250. What is the sale price Marsha will pay?

Answer: _____

2. The table shows books that are on sale at Shelton's Books. If Guy buys 1 book from each genre, what will be his total cost before tax?

Genre	Original Price	Discount
History	$18.00	35%
Mystery	$22.00	15%
Romance	$25.00	10%
Thriller	$12.00	10%

Answer: _____

Name

1. Look at the models below. Which model represents 4^2?

Ⓐ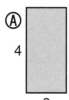
4
2

Ⓑ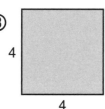
4
4

Ⓒ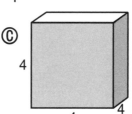
4
4
4

Ⓓ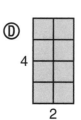
4
2

2. Brett works 40 hours a week at Junior's Smokehouse. He makes $18 an hour. Junior's Smokehouse takes 30% of his pay for taxes and annuity. When Brett cashes his weekly paychecks, how much money will he receive? Write the amount on the check.

JUNIOR'S SMOKEHOUSE
3333 East Lane
Victoria, MI 77482

Check #523

Pay to the Order of ___Brett Jensen___ $ _____

ⓏZEBRA
BANKING
10209, South TX

Mr. Junior
Signature

1. Carlos earns $15 an hour for a 40-hour week and $22.75 an hour for overtime. Carlos worked 48 hours during one week. Which expression can be used to find his salary for that week?

Ⓐ (48 × $15) + (8 × $22.75)   Ⓒ (40 × $15) + (8 × $22.75)

Ⓑ 48 × $22.75   Ⓓ (48 × $15) + (48 × $22.75)

2. Melvin and Sheri bought $5\frac{1}{4}$ tons of hay for their cattle. Because of the drought, they have already used $3\frac{1}{3}$ tons of hay due to the lack of grass. How much hay do Melvin and Sheri have left for their cattle?

Answer: _____

1. Chandler has 168 marbles. He gave $\frac{1}{2}$ of his marbles to his best friend. He then gave $\frac{1}{4}$ of the remaining marbles to his sister. How many marbles does Chandler have left?

Answer: _____

2. Divide the fractions below to find the correct answer to each problem.

A. $3 \div \frac{2}{4} =$ **C.** $7 \div \frac{3}{5} =$

B. $3 \div \frac{2}{5} =$ **D.** $2 \div \frac{3}{4} =$

1. Use the distributive property to simplify the expression.

$$9(8a - 4)$$

2. Solve the problems below.

A. $(-5)^3 =$ _____

B. $(-6)^2 =$ _____

C. $(-3)^3 =$ _____

1. Look at the numbers below. Tell if the numbers are rational or irrational in the space provided.

A. 1.5 _____

C. 0.3333 _____

B. 7 _____

D. $\sqrt{2}$ _____

2. Four students were asked to find the greatest common factor (GCF) of 108 and 420. The table shows their answers. Which student did this correctly?

Ⓐ Peta

Ⓑ Perry

Ⓒ Katie

Ⓓ George

Name	Answer
George	18
Peta	6
Katie	12
Perry	9

Name

1. Jody is mowing his field of $2\frac{1}{3}$ acres for hay. One morning, Jody mows half the field. If Jody plans on mowing the rest of the field in the afternoon, what is the number of acres Jody still needs to mow?

Ⓐ $1\frac{1}{3}$ acres

Ⓒ $1\frac{2}{3}$ acres

Ⓑ $1\frac{1}{6}$ acres

Ⓓ $1\frac{5}{6}$ acres

2. Patricia wants to buy a new video game. She opens her piggy bank and counts her money. Patricia finds she has $35 worth of dimes. The equation below can be used to solve for d, the number of dimes Patricia has. Based on the equation, which of the following describes a way to solve for d? Solve for d.

Ⓐ Multiply both sides by 0.10.

Ⓑ Add 0.10 to both sides.

Ⓒ Divide both sides by 0.10.

Ⓓ Subtract 0.10 from both sides.

$$0.10d = 35$$

$$d = \underline{\hspace{2cm}}$$

Name

1. Mrs. Lee is buying rulers to put into a container for her students. A package of rulers contains 8 rulers and costs $1.89. In each package, 2 of the rulers are blue, 2 rulers are red, 2 rulers are orange, and 2 rulers are yellow. The container has the capacity to hold 90 rulers. What is the least number of packages Mrs. Lee can buy in order to fill the container?

Answer: _____

2. Write the correct vocabulary word from the word bank for each definition.

> **Word Bank**
>
> percent   integer   irrational   reciprocal   proportion

A. one of two numbers whose product is 1 _____

B. ratio of a number to 100 or "per one hundred" _____

C. one of the set of whole numbers and their opposites _____

D. an equation that states that two ratios are equivalent _____

E. a number that can't be expressed as a simple fraction _____

1. Rebecca won $2,000 on a scratch-off lottery ticket. She deposited the $2,000 into a savings account with a simple interest rate of 6% per year. How much interest will Rebecca earn in 5 years?

Answer: _____

2. For Michael's birthday, his mother bought him a video game system that cost $420, a new video game for $58.28, and an extra controller for $32.45 so his younger brother could also play. Sales tax is 8.25%. How much will Michael's mother pay for the items?

Answer: _____

1. Two friends are playing a game of numbers. The object of the game is to pick three cards that have the same value. It's now Hank's turn. If he picks the correct cards, he wins the game. Looking at the cards below, which card should Hank **not** pick?

   Ⓐ Card 1

   Ⓑ Card 2

   Ⓒ Card 3

   Ⓓ Card 4

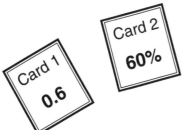
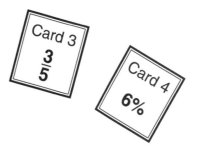

Card 1 **0.6**

Card 2 **60%**

Card 3 **$\frac{3}{5}$**

Card 4 **6%**

2. Look at the table of fractions with decimal and percent equivalents. Which column is **not** correct?

   Ⓐ A   Ⓒ C

   Ⓑ B   Ⓓ D

	A	B	C	D
Fraction	$\frac{1}{2}$	$\frac{1}{3}$	$\frac{2}{3}$	$\frac{1}{4}$
Decimal	0.5	0.333…	0.166…	0.25
Percentage	50%	33.33%	66.67%	25%

Name

1. After teaching his class what a rational number is, Mr. Bozalina asked what kind of answer results when a rational number is multiplied by zero? If his students answered correctly, what answer below did they give?

    Ⓐ The answer is 4 more than the original number.

    Ⓑ The answer stays the same as the original number.

    Ⓒ The answer is zero.

    Ⓓ The answer depends on if the original number has a positive or negative sign.

2. Look at the fractions below. Compare each pair of fractions by shading in the parts equivalent to the fractions. Then, use inequality symbols to compare the fractions.

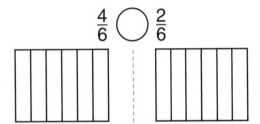

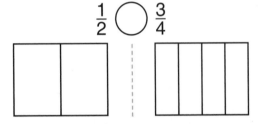

Name

1. Four students wrote numbers in scientific notation form on the board. Which student wrote the number with the greatest value?

    Ⓐ Kenny

    Ⓑ Trisha

    Ⓒ Garth

    Ⓓ George

Student	Scientific Notation
George	9.8×10^{-3}
Kenny	7.6×10^{-4}
Garth	6.7×10^4
Trisha	8.9×10^3

2. A teacher wrote the expression below on the board. She asked four groups of students to simplify the expression. Which group answered the problem correctly?

$$(6^2 - 2^4) \cdot \sqrt{16}$$

Ⓐ	Ⓑ	Ⓒ	Ⓓ
Group 1	**Group 2**	**Group 3**	**Group 4**
108	16	64	80

Warm-Up 1
1. B   2. $25.50

Warm-Up 2
1. C   2. D

Warm-Up 3
1. A   2. 4

Warm-Up 4
1. A   2. A

Warm-Up 5
1. D   2. $112.00

Warm-Up 6
1. $m = 24$ 2. $25.10

Warm-Up 7
1. B   2. C

Warm-Up 8
1. C   2. B

Warm-Up 9
1. B   2. $1.74

Warm-Up 10
1. A   2. $\frac{3}{5}$

Warm-Up 11
1. C   2. C

Warm-Up 12
1. A   2. B

Warm-Up 13
1. $(9 \times 10) - (11 \times 8)$
2. 126 miles

Warm-Up 14
1. 5 boxes   2. $20.63

Warm-Up 15
1. C   2. C

Warm-Up 16
1. $34.56   2. $\frac{5}{10} = \frac{1}{2}$

Warm-Up 17
1. 270,556   2. 6.32 hours

Warm-Up 18
1. 60 hours   2. B

Warm-Up 19
1. A. <   C. >
   B. <   D. <
2. C

Warm-Up 20
1. 30 minutes   2. D

Warm-Up 21
1. D   2. D

Warm-Up 22
1. C   2. C

Warm-Up 23
1. 7 books   2. B

Warm-Up 24
1. D   2. D

Warm-Up 25
1. C   2. 5 minutes

Warm-Up 26
1. $143.13   2. C

Warm-Up 27
1. $4.50   2. $579.31

Warm-Up 28
1. 75% and $\frac{3}{4}$
2. 33%

Warm-Up 29
1. 70   2. A

Warm-Up 30
1. D   2. **% Correct (Greatest to Least)**

Elia	97.78 %
James	73.33 %
Tyler	64.44 %
EJ	55.56 %

Warm-Up 31
1. 83.33%
2. Possible Answers:

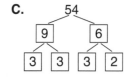

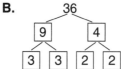

Warm-Up 32
1. A. >   C. <
   B. <
2. C

Warm-Up 33
1. $600
2. **A.** 62,015   **C.** 54,165
   B. 30,615   **D.** 69,865

Warm-Up 34
1. $525.30   2. $1.80

Warm-Up 35
1. A   2. A

Warm-Up 36
1. 2.24 gigabytes   2. 7

Warm-Up 37
1. C   2. A

Warm-Up 38
1. $6,116   2. $2,397 profit

Warm-Up 39
1. C   2. $19x + 18$

Warm-Up 40
1. $65x + 21$ 2. C

Warm-Up 41
1. D; 20   2. A; 61

Warm-Up 42
1. A   2. $\frac{6}{40} = \frac{3}{20}$

Warm-Up 43
1. C   2. B

Warm-Up 44
1. 150 marbles   2. B

Warm-Up 45
1. 20 balls   2. D

Warm-Up 46
1. 390 buttons   2. 257 seashells

Warm-Up 47
1. $19.20   2. A; 65

Warm-Up 48
1. D   2. B

Warm-Up 49
1. **Distributive Property** lets you multiply a sum by a factor by multiplying each addend separately and then adding the products.
   Example: $5(x + 2) = 5 \cdot x + 5 \cdot 2$

   Commutative Property lets you change the order of the operands without changing the results (addition or multiplication). Example: $2 \times 5 = 5 \times 2$
2. 10 inches

Warm-Up 50
1. B
2. **A.** 150   **B.** 45

Warm-Up 51
1. $62.50   2. $63.70

Warm-Up 52
1. B   2. $504.00

Warm-Up 53
1. C   2. $1\frac{11}{12}$ tons

Warm-Up 54
1. 63 marbles
2. **A.** 6   **C.** $11\frac{2}{3}$
   B. $7\frac{1}{2}$ **D.** $2\frac{2}{3}$

Warm-Up 55
1. $72a - 36$
2. **A.** -125   **C.** -27
   B. 36

Warm-Up 56
1. **A.** rational   **C.** rational
   B. rational   **D.** irrational
2. C

Warm-Up 57
1. B   2. C; $d = 350$

Warm-Up 58
1. 12 packages
2. **A.** reciprocal   **C.** integer   **E.** irrational
   B. percent   **D.** proportion

Warm-Up 59
1. $600   2. $552.87

Warm-Up 60
1. D   2. C

Warm-Up 61
1. C
2.

Warm-Up 62
1. C   2. D

Measurement and Geometry

Name

1. Look at the angles. If $\angle XYZ = 63.6°$, what is the angle of its supplement?

Ⓐ 180°

Ⓑ 116.4°

Ⓒ 90°

Ⓓ 63.6°

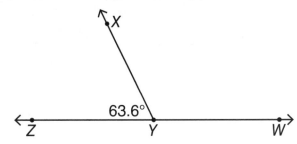

2. Which statement below is true about complementary angles?

Ⓐ Complementary angles are two angles with a sum of 180°.

Ⓑ Complementary angles are two angles with a sum of 145°.

Ⓒ Complementary angles are two angles with a sum of 90°.

Ⓓ Complementary angles are two angles with a sum of 80°.

Name

1. Scott drew a triangle on the coordinate plane below. What are the coordinates for point *B*?

Ⓐ (-3, 4)

Ⓑ (4, 4)

Ⓒ (-4, -4)

Ⓓ (3, 4)

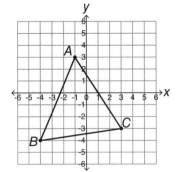

2. Which formula below will give the circumference of the circle?

Ⓐ $C = π \cdot 15^2$

Ⓑ $C = 15 \cdot π \cdot 2$

Ⓒ $C = 15 \cdot 2$

Ⓓ $C = 15 \cdot 15$

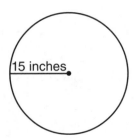

15 inches

Name

1. Beverly drew a shape on the coordinate plane. What is the area, in square units, of the shaded region Beverly drew?

Ⓐ 25 square units

Ⓑ 24 square units

Ⓒ 23 square units

Ⓓ 22 square units

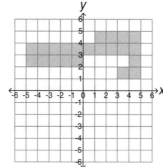

2. Which shape below is an isosceles triangle?

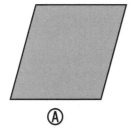  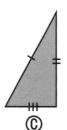 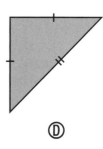

Ⓐ   Ⓑ   Ⓒ   Ⓓ

Name

1. Melvin changes the oil in his truck every 3,000 miles. He uses a pail in the shape of a cylinder that has a height of 2 feet and a radius of 1 foot. What is the approximate surface area?

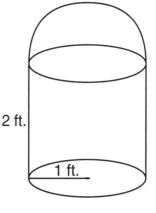

2 ft.

1 ft.

Answer: _____

2. Look at the two angles below. Fill in the blank in the sentence based on the angles.

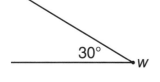

30°
w

150°
z

∠w and ∠z are _____ angles.

1. Which statement about a rhombus is *not* true?

Ⓐ Both pairs of opposite sides are parallel.

Ⓑ All sides are congruent.

Ⓒ Consecutive angles are complementary angles.

Ⓓ Both pairs of opposite angles are congruent.

2. What are the coordinates for the triangle point and the cross point?

Triangle point: _____

Cross point: _____

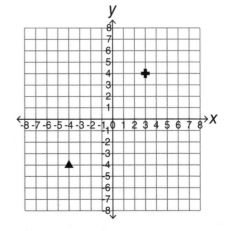

1. Look at the ruler. How long is the paintbrush to the nearest sixteenth of an inch?

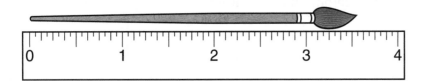

Answer: _____

2. Which diagram is labeled correctly?

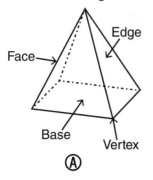 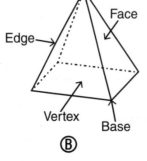 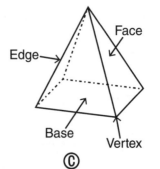 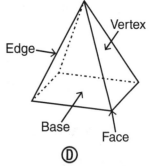

Ⓐ   Ⓑ   Ⓒ   Ⓓ

Name

1. Margo is a veterinarian at a zoo, and she is working with a sick elephant. If she needs to find the weight of the elephant, which unit of measurement would be the best?

Ⓐ ounces

Ⓒ tons

Ⓑ feet

Ⓓ pounds

2. In a geometry class, Mrs. Rhombus drew a triangle on the board. She told her class that the sum of the first 2 angles was 140°. She challenged her students to find which statement from below would give the measurement of the third angle.

Ⓐ Add 140° twice, and then subtract from 360° to get the measurement of the third angle.

Ⓑ Subtract 140° from 180°. That will give the measurement of the third angle.

Ⓒ Add 140° and 180°. That will give the measurement of the third angle.

Ⓓ Subtract 140° from 360°. That will give the measurement of the third angle.

Name

1. Which three-dimensional figure is represented by the net shown below?

Ⓐ hexagonal square

Ⓑ hexagonal prism

Ⓒ windmill prism

Ⓓ pentagonal prism

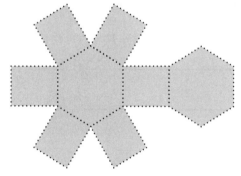

2. Which statement is true about a triangular prism?

Ⓐ A triangular prism has 6 faces.

Ⓑ A triangular prism has 5 faces.

Ⓒ A triangular prism has 4 faces.

Ⓓ A triangular prism has 8 faces.

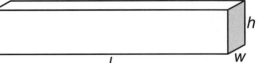

Daily Warm-Up **9**

1. Janice is trying to find a formula to get the volume of the rectangular prism below. Which answer choice is correct?

   Ⓐ $l + w + h$

   Ⓒ $l - w - h$

   Ⓑ $l \times w \times h$

   Ⓓ $3l \times 3w \times 4h$

2. Classify the shapes using the table below. Write the name of the shape, and the number of faces, edges, and vertices for each.

  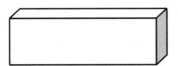 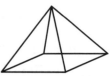

Shape Name	Faces	Edges	Vertices

Daily Warm-Up **10**

1. A teacher drew a transversal line crossing parallel lines. Lines *w* and *x* are parallel. If $\angle 1 = 45°$, then find the angle measure for $\angle 7$.

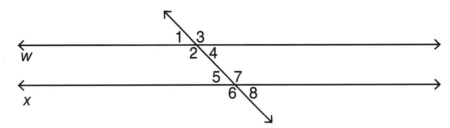

   Answer: _____

2. Jennifer drew a shape on the board that has 12 edges. Which answer choice below could be the shape that Jennifer drew?

   Ⓐ cone

   Ⓒ cube or rectangular prism

   Ⓑ square pyramid

   Ⓓ triangular prism

80

Name

1. Which statement about a translation is *true*?

Ⓐ A translation creates a mirror image across a particular line.

Ⓑ A translation slides a point or figure to a new location.

Ⓒ A translation is a fixed point.

Ⓓ A translation does nothing.

2. In Mrs. Young's science lab, she has a cylindrical container filled with water. The container has a volume of 8.75 liters. What is the volume of the container in milliliters?

Answer: _____

Name

1. Mary has a button on her coat that has a radius of 4 millimeters. What is the diameter of the button on Mary's coat?

Answer: _____

2. Chandler won a medal for selling the most bags of popcorn for a fundraiser at school. The medal has a radius of 5 centimeters. What is the medal's diameter?

Answer: _____

Name

1. Look at the figure below. What is the volume of the cylinder? Round your answer to the nearest hundredth.

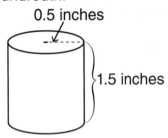

0.5 inches

1.5 inches

Answer: _____

2. Andy's teacher drew the diagram below on the board as a homework problem for her students. The teacher asked each student to find the measure for angle *m*. If her students did this correctly, what answer did they give?

Ⓐ 98°

Ⓑ 82°

Ⓒ 56°

Ⓓ 42°

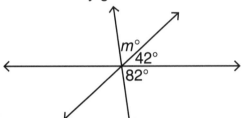

Name

1. Garland weighed a bag of rice and found how many grams the bag weighed. Garland needs to convert the measurement from grams to kilograms. Which answer choice below will give Garland the answer?

Ⓐ Multiply by $\dfrac{1\ kg}{1{,}000\ g}$

Ⓒ Multiply by $\dfrac{100\ kg}{1}$

Ⓑ Multiply by $\dfrac{1{,}000\ kg}{1\ g}$

Ⓓ Multiply by $\dfrac{1\ g}{100\ g}$

2. Ethan lives 14.6 miles from the nearest store. How many feet is it from Ethan's house to the store and back?

Answer: _____

Name

1. Lettilyn drew the two shapes below. The two shapes are similar. She asked Lawrence to find the length of the base of the smaller triangle. If Lawrence did this correctly, which answer did he give?

Ⓐ 18 cm

Ⓑ 14 cm

Ⓒ 12 cm

Ⓓ 9 cm

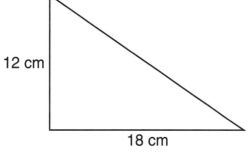

12 cm

18 cm

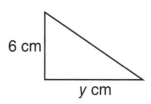

6 cm

y cm

2. Kendall drew the triangle below. Answer the questions concerning Kendall's drawing.

Find the area of the triangle. _____

Find the perimeter for the triangle. _____

What type of triangle is this? _____

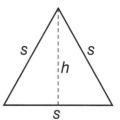

s   s

h

s

s = 6.5 ft.   h = 5.6 ft.

Name

1. Randy drew a map of the block he lives on. Which is true about the map?

Ⓐ Line $\overline{WZ}$ is perpendicular to line $\overline{XY}$.

Ⓑ Line $\overline{WZ}$ is parallel to line $\overline{XY}$.

Ⓒ Line $\overline{WX}$ is parallel to $\overline{XY}$.

Ⓓ Line $\overline{WZ}$ is perpendicular to $\overline{WY}$.

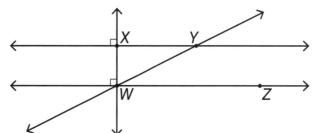

2. Cameron built the rectangular prism below out of 1-inch blocks he got for his birthday. What is the number of blocks he used?

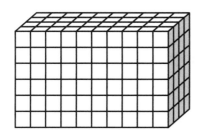

Answer: _____

Name

1. Sheri drew a square on a poster board. The square had an area of 85 square feet. Which answer choice would be the best approximate length for each side of the square?

Ⓐ 9.9 ft.   Ⓑ 9.2 ft.   Ⓒ 9 ft.   Ⓓ 8.8 ft.

2. Marco marked a point in the second quadrant of a coordinate plane. Which set of coordinates could be Marco's point?

Ⓐ (5, 5)   Ⓒ (-2, -2)

Ⓑ (-4, 2)   Ⓓ (1, -5)

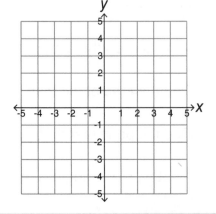

Name

1. A teacher is working with a small group of students. She asked each of the four students to describe a polygon. According to the table, which student gave the best definition?

Ⓐ Kristi

Ⓑ David

Ⓒ Kevin

Ⓓ Kathy

Student	Answer
Kathy	a closed figure
Kristi	a closed figure made up of three or more sides
David	an open figure
Kevin	a shape with only 2 sides

2. Which statement about an isosceles triangle is *true*?

Ⓐ An isosceles triangle has more than 6 sides.

Ⓑ An isosceles triangle has 3 sides of different lengths.

Ⓒ An isosceles triangle has 2 congruent sides.

Ⓓ An isosceles triangle has 2 bases and 4 sides.

Name

1. Hank is trying to find the perimeter of a rectangle. Which answer choice below will help Hank find the answer?

Ⓐ $P = 2l + 2w$

Ⓒ $P = lwh$

Ⓑ $P = \frac{1}{2}bh$

Ⓓ $P = l \times 3.14$

2. When Connie drew two angles, the teacher told her that two angles are _____ angles if the sum of their angles measures 90 degrees.

Ⓐ supplementary

Ⓒ obtuse

Ⓑ complementary

Ⓓ right

Name

1. What is the area and perimeter of the parallelogram shown?

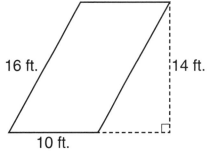

Area = _____

Perimeter = _____

2. What term describes a straight line from a point on a circle to the midpoint of the circle?

Ⓐ circumference

Ⓑ integer

Ⓒ radius

Ⓓ diameter

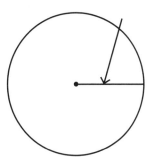

1. Mindy drew the similar shapes below on a sheet of paper. Find the length of $\overline{RT}$.

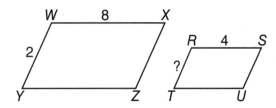

Answer: _____

2. Dana drew a circle that had a diameter of 15 cm. What is the circumference?

Ⓐ 176.63 cm

Ⓑ 47.16 cm

Ⓒ 47.10 cm

Ⓓ 23.55 cm

1. Look at the circles. Find the circumference and area of each circle.

Circle A

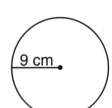

C = _____

A = _____

Circle B

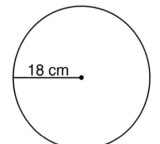

C = _____

A = _____

2. Coach Parson is teaching his students about the game of basketball in his physical education class. The basketball he is using has a circumference of 30 inches. What is the diameter of the basketball rounded to the nearest tenth?

Ⓐ 9.6 inches

Ⓑ 6.2 inches

Ⓒ 4.8 inches

Ⓓ 3.1 inches

1. Randy is mowing his rectangular-shaped back yard. The back yard is 15 yards wide and 20 yards long. What is the area of the back yard Randy is mowing?

Ⓐ 600 square yards

Ⓑ 300 square yards

Ⓒ 150 square yards

Ⓓ 60 square yards

2. Four students wrote properties that describe a cube. Which friend did this correctly?

Ⓐ Steward

Ⓑ Peggy

Ⓒ Frank

Ⓓ Stephanie

Friend	Definition
Steward	6 faces, 8 vertices, and 8 edges
Stephanie	8 faces, 6 vertices, and 12 edges
Peggy	8 faces, 8 vertices, and 12 edges
Frank	6 faces, 8 vertices, and 12 edges

1. Look at the transformation on the grid. Which transformation is modeled below?

Ⓐ slide

Ⓑ reflection

Ⓒ rotation

Ⓓ translation

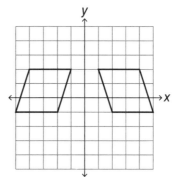

2. Using 2-dimensional figures, Cindy created the 3-dimensional figure shown below. Which answer choice identifies the shapes she used?

Ⓐ 1 square and 2 rectangles

Ⓑ 2 squares and 3 rectangles

Ⓒ 2 squares and 4 rectangles

Ⓓ 2 squares and 2 rectangles

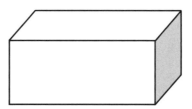

Name

1. Four groups of students were asked to describe the properties that describe a triangular pyramid. Which group did this correctly?

Ⓐ Group 1

Ⓑ Group 2

Ⓒ Group 3

Ⓓ Group 4

Group	Answer
Group 1	4 faces, 4 vertices, and 3 edges
Group 2	4 faces, 4 vertices, and 6 edges
Group 3	3 faces, 6 vertices, and 6 edges
Group 4	3 faces, 6 vertices, and 3 edges

2. Terry drinks 5 glasses of water each day. Each glass holds $1\frac{1}{2}$ cups of water. How many fluid ounces of water has she consumed during a 5-day period?

Answer: _____

Name

1. Identify the angles below.

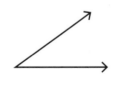 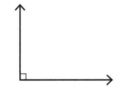 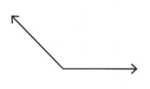

_____   _____   _____

2. Look at the diagram below. Which expression can be used to find the angle measure of ∠wxz?

Ⓐ 180 + 129

Ⓑ 180 ÷ 129

Ⓒ 180 − 129

Ⓓ 180 × 129

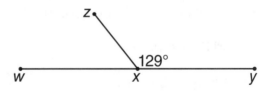

Name

1. Which is the best unit of measure for the volume of a kitchen sink?

(A) ounces   (C) gallons

(B) cups   (D) quarts

2. Draw an angle that would be the supplementary angle to the one in the box. What type of angle would it be?

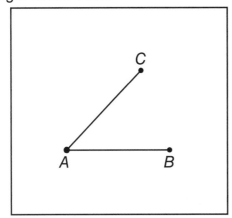

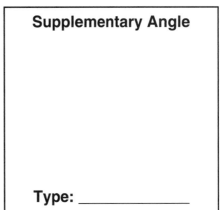

Supplementary Angle

Type: _____

Name

1. Rosa drew the shape below. She asked Hannah to find the measuremen of ∠M. If Hannah answered correctly, what answer did she give?

(A) 360°

(B) 180°

(C) 145°

(D) 45°

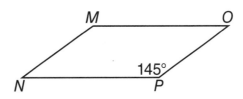

2. Terry used $1\frac{1}{4}$ cups of milk for her first recipe. She used $1\frac{1}{2}$ cups in her second recipe. How many ounces of milk did Terry use all together?

Answer: _____

1. A teacher asked his students, "What unit of measure is a metric unit for mass?" Henry raised his hand and answered correctly with one of the answers below. Which answer did Henry choose?

Ⓐ kilometers

Ⓒ meters

Ⓑ centimeters

Ⓓ grams

2. While doing a science experiment in her science lab, Mrs. Chilek used four liter-sized bottles for the experiment. She filled each of them with water. How many milliliters of water did it take to fill the 4 containers?

Answer: _____

1. Margaret has 6 gallons of white paint. How many pints of white paint does Margaret have?

Answer: _____

2. Mark drew a shape on a coordinate plane. The shape's coordinates are (-3, -5). In which quadrant did Mark draw the shape?

Ⓐ Quadrant I

Ⓑ Quadrant II

Ⓒ Quadrant III

Ⓓ Quadrant IV

Name

1. Which diagram is labeled correctly?

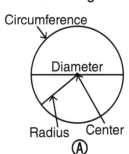 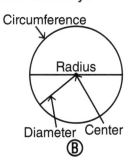 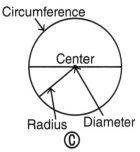 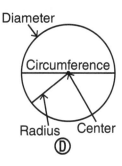

2. Andrew bought a plastic container in the shape of a rectangular prism. He wants to know the volume of the container to see if he can use it to store his breakfast cereal. What is the volume of the rectangular prism?

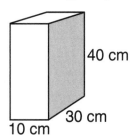

Answer: _____

Name

1. Identify the three triangles below.

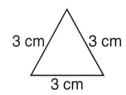 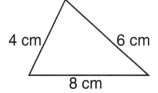 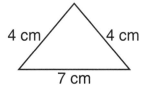

_____ _____ _____

2. Which answer choice represents complementary angles?

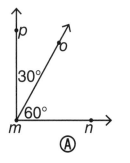 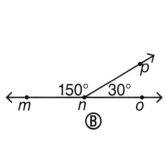 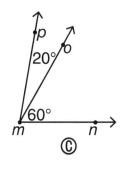 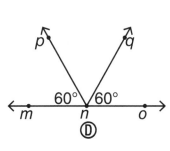

1. Wanda's grandmother made her a tablecloth for her new table. The table has a circumference of 18 feet and is made from cedar. What is the area of the table rounded to the nearest hundredth?

Answer: _____

2. In Mrs. Chilek's science lab, students weighed objects that were equivalent to 2.5 kilograms. Which answer choice is equivalent to 2.5 kilograms?

Ⓐ 25 grams

Ⓒ 2,500 grams

Ⓑ 500 grams

Ⓓ 25,000 grams

1. Lee drew a right triangle on a sheet of paper. He marked two sides of the triangle as 9 centimeters and 12 centimeters. What is the length of the hypotenuse?

Answer: _____

2. In an attempt to eat healthier, Gordon is growing a vegetable garden. The garden is going to be a rectangular shape, 7 feet long and 5 feet wide. What is the perimeter of the garden Gordon is making?

Ⓐ 12 feet   Ⓑ 19 feet   Ⓒ 24 feet   Ⓓ 35 feet

Name

1. Jason's mom bought a bunch of bananas for the banana nut bread she is planning to make over the weekend. The bunch of bananas weighed a total of 96 ounces. What is the weight of the bunch of bananas in pounds?

Answer: _____

2. Look at the figures on the grid. What type of transformation is happening?

Ⓐ reflection of 5 units

Ⓑ translation of 4 units

Ⓒ translation of 5 units

Ⓓ reflection of 4 units

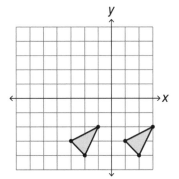

Name

1. Look at the square shown below. How many lines of symmetry does the square have?

Ⓐ 8

Ⓑ 4

Ⓒ 2

Ⓓ 0

2. Louis drew a reflection on a coordinate plane. What is the reflection across the *x*-axis of the point (-4, -3)?

Ⓐ (-4, 3)

Ⓑ (4, -3)

Ⓒ (4, 3)

Ⓓ (3, 4)

1. Derek poured a glass of water after practicing dancing with his partner Kelly. The base of the glass had a diameter of 5 centimeters. What is the circumference of the base of the glass?

Answer: _____

2. Mark has a box that is in the shape of a rectangular prism. The box has a length of 17 inches, a width of 10.2 inches, and a height of 2 inches. He plans to use the box at Christmas. What is the volume of the box in cubic inches?

Answer: _____

1. Look at the diagram. Find the measurement for each angle. The first one is done for you.

∠MOQ = 112°

∠NOP = _____ °

∠POQ = _____ °

∠MON = _____ °

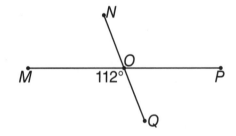

2. Look at the circle. Complete the statements by filling in the corresponding letters. The first one is done for you.

N is the center.

_____ is the diameter.

_____ and _____ are the radii.

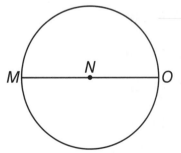

1. Look at the rectangular prism. What is the volume in cubic inches?

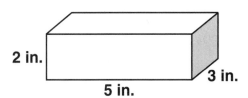

2 in.

3 in.

5 in.

Answer: _____

2. Austin drew the right triangle shown below. What is the length of $\overline{WQ}$?

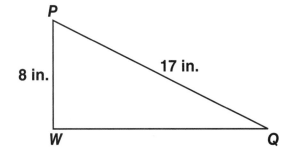

P

8 in.

17 in.

W   Q

Answer: _____

1. Chandler received an above-ground swimming pool for his birthday. The swimming pool has a radius of 4 feet. What is the circumference of the swimming pool Chandler received for his birthday?

Ⓐ $8\pi^2$ feet

Ⓒ 8π feet

Ⓑ $4\pi^2$ feet

Ⓓ 4π feet

2. A teacher asked Rebecca to come to the board and draw a figure in quadrant I, and then show its translation over the *x*-axis. If Rebecca did this correctly, what answer choice did she draw?

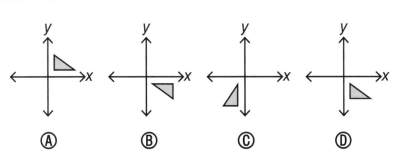

Ⓐ   Ⓑ   Ⓒ   Ⓓ

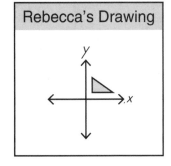

Rebecca's Drawing

Daily
Warm-Up **41**

1. Look at the house.

- The 1s represent some right angles on the house.

- The 2s represent some acute angles on the house.

- The 3s represent _____ .

2. Susan can't remember the geometry problem the teacher wrote on the board. She knows the lengths of two sides of a right triangle were given, but she can't remember the length of the hypotenuse. Which answer choice is the correct length of the hypotenuse rounded to the nearest tenth?

Ⓐ 84.5 km   Ⓒ 13 km

Ⓑ 17 km   Ⓓ 5.8 km

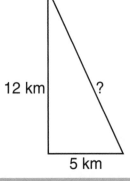

Daily
Warm-Up **42**

1. Complete the statements below.

- A quadrilateral is a _____ with _____ sides.

- A parallelogram has two pairs of sides that are _____ , and opposite angles that are equal.

2. Find the length of the hypotenuse of the triangle below.

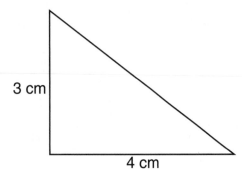

Answer: _____

Name

1. Mrs. Ezell, a science teacher, is using a cylindrical container with a radius of 2 feet. The container has a height of 3 feet. What is the volume of the container rounded to the nearest hundredth?

Answer: _____

2. Look at the model below. What is the volume of the rectangular prism?

Ⓐ 12 cubic centimeters

Ⓑ 46 cubic centimeters

Ⓒ 48 cubic centimeters

Ⓓ 96 cubic centimeters

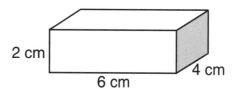

2 cm
6 cm
4 cm

Name

1. Look at the circle. Find the area and circumference of the circle.

Area = _____

Circumference = _____

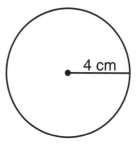

4 cm

2. Patricia drew the parallelogram shown below. She knows the parallelogram has a perimeter of 24 inches. She asked her sister, "Based on the dimensions shown, what is the length of side $\overline{WX}$?" If her sister answered correctly, what answer did she give?

Ⓐ 9.5 inches

Ⓑ 9 inches

Ⓒ 7 inches

Ⓓ 4.8 inches

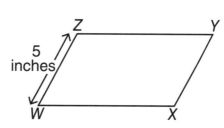

Z   Y
5 inches
W   X

1. Sue bought an aquarium in the shape of a rectangular prism. What is the surface area of the aquarium?

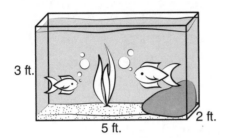

3 ft.

5 ft.

2 ft.

Answer: _____

2. Look at the circle. Points *A*, *B*, *C*, *D*, *E*, and *F* are all on the circle. Which line segment is the diameter of the circle?

Ⓐ $\overline{EZ}$

Ⓒ $\overline{ZA}$

Ⓑ $\overline{FC}$

Ⓓ $\overline{DB}$

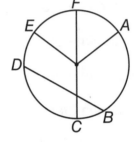

1. A teacher asked her students to identify which term best describes the relationship between the two angles described in the box, complementary or supplementary. The choices below are their responses. Which answer is correct?

Ⓐ supplementary

Ⓑ complementary

Ⓒ both supplementary and complementary

Ⓓ neither supplementary nor complementary

∠x measures 45° and
∠y measures 45°

2. If ∠1 is complementary to ∠2, and ∠2 measures 65°, what is the measure of ∠1?

Ⓐ 25°   Ⓑ 30°   Ⓒ 40°   Ⓓ 90°

Name _____

1. Look at the scalene triangle shown below. Which statement about the triangle is true?

   Ⓐ At least two sides are congruent.

   Ⓑ All three sides are congruent.

   Ⓒ No sides are congruent.

   Ⓓ All three angles are congruent.

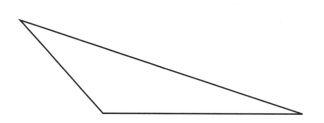

2. Frank drew a rhombus on the board. He then wrote four facts about the rhombus. Which fact about a rhombus is *not* true?

   Ⓐ Fact 1

   Ⓑ Fact 2

   Ⓒ Fact 3

   Ⓓ Fact 4

   > Fact 1: Both pairs of opposite sides are parallel.
   >
   > Fact 2: All angles are right angles.
   >
   > Fact 3: Consecutive angles are supplementary.
   >
   > Fact 4: Both pairs of opposite angles are congruent.

Name _____

1. Which is longer, 10 yards or 425 inches?

   Answer: _____

2. Jennifer is jogging each day for exercise. She runs 2 miles on Monday and $3\frac{1}{2}$ miles on Tuesday. How many more feet did Jennifer run on Tuesday than on Monday?

   Answer: _____

1. Look at the shape below. Which of the answer choices is a formula for finding the area of a parallelogram?

Ⓐ $l \times w$

Ⓑ $b \times$ altitude

Ⓒ $s \times s \times s^2$

Ⓓ $\frac{1}{2} \times (b_1 + b_2) \times h$

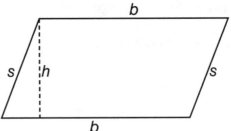

2. Mark cut two circles out of poster board for an art project. The larger circle had a radius of 5 inches. The smaller circle had a radius of 3 inches. What is the difference in their circumferences?

Answer: _____

1. Terry had her husband cut 2 wooden doorstops for their home. The doorstops are in the shape of right triangles and are similar. Look at the doorstops below. Find m, the length of side $\overline{DE}$.

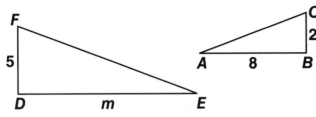

Answer: _____

2. Samantha is on the swim team at school. Her goal is to be an Olympic gold medalist. She swims laps each day at home in her swimming pool. The rectangular pool has a perimeter of 50 feet. The pool has a width of 7 feet. What is the area of the swimming pool?

Answer: _____

Name

1. At the doctor's office, the waiting room is being remodeled. The rectangular room that measures 22 feet by 18 feet will have wooden floors. What is the minimum amount of wooden flooring the doctor will need to buy to complete the office?

Ⓐ 3,564 sq. yd. of wooden flooring

Ⓒ 44 sq. yd. of wooden flooring

Ⓑ 720 sq. yd. of wooden flooring

Ⓓ 4 sq. yd. of wooden flooring

2. Which table shows the number of edges, faces, and vertices a square pyramid has?

Ⓐ

Square Pyramid		
Faces	Edges	Vertices
6	8	5

Ⓒ

Square Pyramid		
Faces	Edges	Vertices
5	8	5

Ⓑ

Square Pyramid		
Faces	Edges	Vertices
5	6	5

Ⓓ

Square Pyramid		
Faces	Edges	Vertices
5	4	3

Name

1. Find the value of ∠c in the complementary angle below.

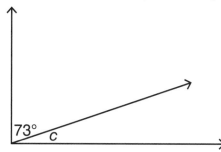

73°
c

∠c = _____ °

2. Marcus asked his mother how much water would fill the bathtub. Which answer choice is the best estimate of the volume of the bathtub?

Ⓐ 50 liters

Ⓒ 50 milliliters

Ⓑ 50 gallons

Ⓓ 50 ounces

Name

1. If point G (0, 3) is translated 4 units left, what are the coordinates of the resulting point G?

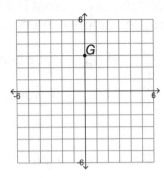

G = (_____ , _____)

2. Which answer choice shows the length of the hypotenuse below?

Ⓐ 15 m

Ⓑ 48 m

Ⓒ 36 m

Ⓓ 10 m

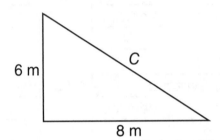

6 m

C

8 m

Name

1. For math class, Ty has to make a geometric shape out of poster board. So far, he has cut out 4 congruent isosceles triangles and 1 square. The sides of the square are congruent to the base of each triangle. He's trying to remember all the 3-dimensional figures he has been taught in math class. What 3-dimensional figure can Ty make using the 1 square and 4 isosceles triangles?

Ⓐ triangular pyramid

Ⓒ triangular prism

Ⓑ square pyramid

Ⓓ square prism

2. A teacher told her class to find the length of the hypotenuse for a triangle with sides of the lengths 5 and 12. If her students did this correctly, which answer below did they give?

Ⓐ 6   Ⓑ 13   Ⓒ 17   Ⓓ not given

Name

1. Chandler has a plastic cube that measures 7 cm on each edge. What is the surface area of his cube? Sketch a drawing in the space below labeling each side of the cube. Then, find the answer.

Answer: _____

2. On a farm, Jack has a large cylinder with a radius of 4 feet and a height of 15 feet. What is the approximate volume of the cylinder Jack has on the farm?

Ⓐ 1,508 cubic feet

Ⓑ 754 cubic feet

Ⓒ 377 cubic feet

Ⓓ 189 cubic feet

Name

1. What type of angle is ∠C?

Ⓐ Right angle   Ⓒ Obtuse angle

Ⓑ Straight angle   Ⓓ Acute angle

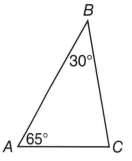

2. Garland drew four shapes on the board. Which shape's pair of angles is **not** supplementary?

   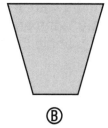      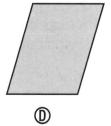

Ⓐ   Ⓑ   Ⓒ   Ⓓ

Name

1. Draw a transformation of the triangle to represent a reflection across the *y*-axis.

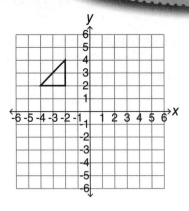

2. Look at the coordinate plane. What geometric shape is located at the coordinates (4, 5)?

Ⓐ cylinder

Ⓒ cube

Ⓑ triangle

Ⓓ parallelogram

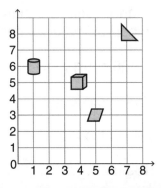

Name

1. Lee is cleaning out his garage. During the cleaning, he finds a wooden box in the shape of a rectangular prism. The container has a white tag on the bottom that gives the dimensions of the wooden box. Lee read that the container has a length of 14 centimeters and a width of 6 centimeters. He can see that the container has a volume of 840 cubic centimeters, but he can't read the measure of the height. What is the height of the box?

Answer: _____

2. Megan was called to the whiteboard in class to draw an angle that measures 65°. Brent was called next to draw an angle supplementary to the angle Megan drew. If they drew their angles correctly, what is the measure of the angle Brent drew?

Answer: _____

Name

1. Wanda Sue is making Christmas wreaths out of sheets of paneling. She cut a circle that has a circumference of 12.56 inches. What is the measurement of the radius of the circle?

Ⓐ 6.28 inches

Ⓑ 4 inches

Ⓒ 3.14 inches

Ⓓ 2 inches

2. Ralph bought a can of soda at a store. The can has a diameter of 64 mm and a height of 12.2 cm. What is the volume of the cylinder in centimeters cubed? Round to the nearest tenth.

Answer: _____

Name

1. After teaching his students about coordinates, a teacher wrote the four sets of coordinates below on the board. He then asked his students which set of coordinates would be found in Quadrant II? If his students answered correctly, which answer choice did they select?

Ⓐ (1, -5)   Ⓒ (-4, 2)

Ⓑ (-2, -6)   Ⓓ (5, 5)

2. Jack drew the rectangles shown below on the board at school. Are the two rectangles similar? Explain your answer.

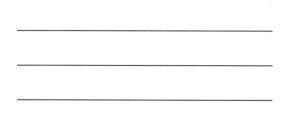
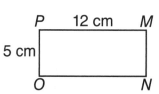
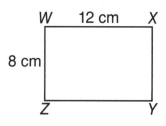

1. Write these measurements of length in order from shortest to longest units of measure.

yards   inches

feet   miles

_____

_____

_____

_____

2. Susanna bought 5 yards of fabric and 3 feet of lace to make a dress for her daughter. How many inches of fabric and lace did Susanna buy all together?

Answer: _____

---

1. Hank wants to take a bath, but the faucet in the tub isn't working. He uses a 2-quart pitcher to fill the tub. How many pitchers of water will Hank need to fill a 50-gallon tub halfway?

Answer: _____

2. Which statement about the term *circumference* is **true**?

Ⓐ The circumference of a circle is a line segment going from the center of the circle to any part of the circle.

Ⓑ The circumference of a circle is the distance around the circle.

Ⓒ The circumference of a circle is a line segment that joins any two points of a circle and passes through the center of the circle.

Ⓓ The circumference of a circle is a set of points in a plane that are the same distance from a given point.

Warm-Up 1
1. B   2. C

Warm-Up 2
1. C   2. B

Warm-Up 3
1. D   2. D

Warm-Up 4
1. 18.84 sq. ft.   2. supplementary

Warm-Up 5
1. C   2. Triangle point: (-4, -4);
Cross point: (3, 4)

Warm-Up 6
1. $3\frac{9}{16}$ inches   2. C

Warm-Up 7
1. C   2. B

Warm-Up 8
1. B   2. B

Warm-Up 9
1. B
2.

Shape Name	Faces	Edges	Vertices
Cube	6	12	8
Triangular Prism	5	9	6
Rectangular Prism	6	12	8
Square Pyramid	5	8	5

Warm-Up 10
1. 135°   2. C

Warm-Up 11
1. B   2. 8,750 milliliters

Warm-Up 12
1. 8 mm   2. 10 cm

Warm-Up 13
1. 1.18 cubic inches   2. C

Warm-Up 14
1. A   2. 154,176 ft.

Warm-Up 15
1. D   2. A = 18.2 sq. ft.
P = 19.5 ft.
equilateral triangle

Warm-Up 16
1. B   2. 240 blocks

Warm-Up 17
1. B   2. B

Warm-Up 18
1. A   2. C

Warm-Up 19
1. A   2. B

Warm-Up 20
1. Area = 140 sq. ft.;
Perimeter = 52 ft.
2. C

Warm-Up 21
1. $\overline{RT}$ = 1   2. C

Warm-Up 22
1. Circle A: C = 56.52 cm; A = 254.34 cm²
Circle B: C = 113.04 cm; A = 1,017.36 cm²
2. A

Warm-Up 23
1. B   2. C

Warm-Up 24
1. B   2. C

Warm-Up 25
1. B   2. 300 ounces

Warm-Up 26
1. acute, right, obtuse   2. C

Warm-Up 27
1. C   2. check drawings; type: obtuse

Warm-Up 28
1. C   2. 22 oz.

Warm-Up 29
1. D
2. 4,000 milliliters

Warm-Up 30
1. 48 pints   2. C

Warm-Up 31
1. A   2. 12,000 cubic centimeters

Warm-Up 32
1. equilateral, scalene, isosceles   2. A

Warm-Up 33
1. 25.86 sq. ft.   2. C

Warm-Up 34
1. 15 cm   2. C

Warm-Up 35
1. 6 pounds   2. B

Warm-Up 36
1. B   2. A

Warm-Up 37
1. 15.7 cm   2. 346.8 cubic inches

Warm-Up 38
1. $\angle NOP = 112°$; $\angle POQ = 68°$; $\angle MON = 68°$
2. $\overline{MO}$ is diameter; $\overline{MN}$ and $\overline{NO}$ are both radii

Warm-Up 39
1. 30 cubic inches   2. 15 inches

Warm-Up 40
1. C   2. D

Warm-Up 41
1. obtuse angles   2. C

Warm-Up 42
1. polygon,   2. 5 cm
   4 sides;
   parallel

Warm-Up 43
1. 37.68 cubic ft.   2. C

Warm-Up 44
1. $A = 50.24$ cm²   2. C
   $C = 25.12$ cm

Warm-Up 45
1. 62 sq. ft.   2. B

Warm-Up 46
1. B   2. A

Warm-Up 47
1. C   2. B

Warm-Up 48
1. 425 inches   2. 7,920 feet

Warm-Up 49
1. B   2. 12.56 inches

Warm-Up 50
1. $m = 20$ 2. 126 sq. ft.

Warm-Up 51
1. C   2. C

Warm-Up 52
1. 17°   2. B

Warm-Up 53
1. (-4, 3)   2. D

Warm-Up 54
1. B   2. B

Warm-Up 55
1. 294 cm²   2. B

Warm-Up 56
1. D   2. B

Warm-Up 57
1.

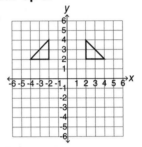

2. C

Warm-Up 58
1. 10 cm   2. 115°

Warm-Up 59
1. D   2. 392.3 cm³

Warm-Up 60
1. C   2. not similar; the sides are
   not proportionate.

Warm-Up 61
1. inches   2. 216 inches
   feet
   yards
   miles

Warm-Up 62
1. 50 pitchers   2. B

Data Analysis and Probability

1. Ty and Maci are playing a game. On Maci's first three spins, she landed on 5. She asked Ty how many times the spinner would land on 5 if she spun 100 times, according to its probability.

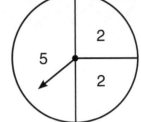

Ⓐ 33 times

Ⓒ 50 times

Ⓑ 25 times

Ⓓ 100 times

2. Sasha is learning about plots. She created her own stem-and-leaf plot using random numbers. Based on her data, what is the **mode** of her numbers?

1	0	2		
2	2	2	3	4
3	2	2	3	4
4	2	2	5	6
5	2	5	7	
6	5	5	5	5

Answer: _____

1. At a video arcade, Cane had 5 tickets numbered 1 through 5. If Cane uses a ticket at random to play a game, what is the probability he will select a ticket with an even number printed on it?

Ⓐ $\frac{3}{5}$

Ⓒ $\frac{2}{5}$

Ⓑ $\frac{1}{2}$

Ⓓ $\frac{1}{5}$

2. At Wharton Junior High, shirts are being sold for Spirit Week. The shirts come in three colors: black, blue, and white. The students can choose from 2 different colors of ink and 2 different styles of font. How many different types of shirts can be made?

Ⓐ 12 types

Ⓑ 10 types

Ⓒ 7 types

Ⓓ 2 types

Name

1. Mindy's washing machine and dryer no longer work. She hasn't bought a new machine in 8 years, so she decides to shop around and get a list of prices. The salesperson gives her the prices of the 8 models of washing machines and dryers they carry. What is the range of the prices Mindy has to choose from?

Ⓐ $1,484

Ⓑ $1,242

Ⓒ $1,356

Ⓓ $1,169

| $1,544 | $1,242 | $1,242 | $2,285 |
| $1,116 | $1,899 | $1,649 | $1,423 |

2. Gretchen is playing a board game with her sister Kim. Gretchen needs to roll a number less than 5 to make it to a safe place on the board. If she rolls a 5 or 6, she will land on "lose a turn" or "go back to start." If Gretchen rolls a six-sided number dice one time, what is the probability it will land on a number less than 5?

Ⓐ 1 out of 3

Ⓒ 2 out of 3

Ⓑ 1 out of 6

Ⓓ 5 out of 6

Name

1. Barry owns a snow-cone shop. He offers 3 different sized cones and 8 different flavors. How many options does a customer have to choose from when ordering a single-flavor cone at Barry's shop?

Ⓐ 48 single flavor options

Ⓑ 24 single flavor options

Ⓒ 11 single flavor options

Ⓓ 3 single flavor options

2. At Perry's Pizza Parlor, employees can either wear blue, red, or white shirts. They can wear jeans or khaki pants. How many total possible uniform combinations are there?

Answer: _____

Name

1. Mr. Sitka wants to compare the amount of money each grade level earned for a school fundraiser so he can report the results at the next faculty meeting. Which option would be the best way for Mr. Sitka to present this data?

Ⓐ pie chart

Ⓒ stem and leaf

Ⓑ line graph

Ⓓ bar graph

2. Today, there is a 30% chance of rain. Tomorrow, the weatherman is calling for a 70% chance of heavy rain and possible hail. The chance of rain tomorrow can best be described as

Ⓐ impossible.

Ⓒ likely.

Ⓑ certain.

Ⓓ not likely.

Name

1. Janice is watching birds. She keeps track of how many birds she sees each day. Based on the data listed below, which box-and-whisker plot represents the data correctly?

79, 87, 89, 91, 93, 93, 95, 100

Ⓐ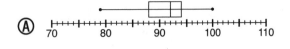

Ⓒ

Ⓑ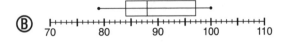

Ⓓ

2. Peggy is trying to come up with a 4-digit PIN for her new debit card. She has come up with 2 odd numbers for her first two digits but wants to use 2 even numbers for the last two digits. How many different 2-digit numbers can Peggy make with the numbers 2, 4, 6, and 8 without using the same digit twice?

Answer: _____

Name

1. Jack is the lead scoring basketball player on the varsity team. The table shows the points he scored in the last eight games. Which number is the lower quartile for this data set?

Ⓐ 17

Ⓒ 23

Ⓑ 18

Ⓓ 31

Game	Points
1	24
2	15
3	19
4	17
5	38
6	21
7	39
8	25

2. Sheri has a job interview. She is trying to decide on what to wear. She has narrowed it down to 3 blouses, 2 pairs of shoes, and 4 skirts. How many different outfits are possible for Sheri to choose from?

Answer: _____

Name

1. Students in 4th and 5th grade took a survey regarding their favorite cafeteria food. What percent of the students selected pizza as their favorite food?

Ⓐ 60%

Ⓑ 40%

Ⓒ 30%

Ⓓ 20%

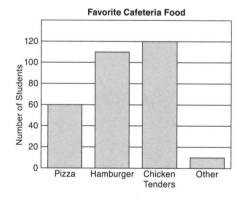

2. Sarah has 1 red die, 1 green die, 1 purple die, and 1 black cube in a bag. Each die and the cube are the same size and shape. If Sarah picks two items from the bag without looking, what is the probability she will pick a red die first and a black cube next?

Ⓐ $\frac{1}{2}$

Ⓑ $\frac{1}{3}$

Ⓒ $\frac{1}{12}$

Ⓓ $\frac{1}{4}$

Name

1. Austin bought his dog Chloe a 5-pound bag of dog food on Monday. For the next 4 days, he fed his dog the same amount of food. Based on the graph, what amount of dog food did Austin feed his dog each day? How much dog food will be left after the fifth day?

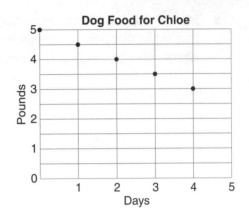

Dog Food for Chloe

Answer: _____

2. Ella and Libby were playing a board game. They played 5 games all together. Ella scored 25, 18, 19, 19, and 24 points, respectively, on each game. Libby scored 21, 21, 24, 24, and 25 on each game. What was each girl's average?

Answer: _____

Name

1. Sara's teacher asked her to write seven numbers on the board that were less than 20. Sara wrote the numbers 3, 6, 5, 4, 8, 9, and 14. Her teacher then asked her to find the mean for the set of data she wrote. If Sara answered correctly, which answer choice did she give?

Ⓐ 7   Ⓒ 4

Ⓑ 6   Ⓓ 3

2. On two of Mark's math tests, he scored 75 and 83. Mark wants to have a mean score of 84. What does Mark have to score on his next test to have a mean of 84?

Answer: _____

Name

1. In Mr. Mai's math class, he is teaching a lesson on probability. He shows the class 15 dimes he had sitting in a jar on his desk. With the help of his class, they recorded the dates printed on the dimes and graphed the data using a bar graph. At random, if Mr. Mai takes 1 dime out of the jar, based on the results on the graph, what is the probability that the date on the dime will be 1970 or earlier?

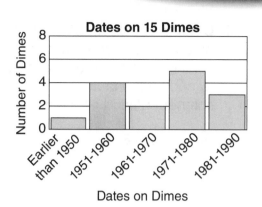

Dates on 15 Dimes

Answer: _____

2. Linda created the table below based on numbers she collected during a 10-day period. Which statement is *true* about the data?

Day	1	2	3	4	5	6	7	8	9	10
Number	15	21	12	8	25	20	18	15	11	15

Ⓐ The mode is 15.

Ⓑ The median is 25.

Ⓒ The range is 15.

Ⓓ The mean is 160.

Name

1. Henry and Sam are playing a game. It's Henry's turn to spin the spinner. Henry needs an even number to win the game. What is the probability that the spinner will land on an even number?

Ⓐ 1

Ⓑ 1 out of 3

Ⓒ 5 out of 6

Ⓓ 2 out of 3

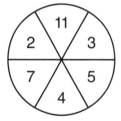

2. Jake collects only green marbles and stores them in a bag. He closes his eyes, reaches into the bag, and grabs 1 marble. Which best describes the chance Jake will choose a marble that is green?

Ⓐ likely

Ⓑ probably

Ⓒ certain

Ⓓ possible

Name

1. Cindy was playing a board game. She wondered what number the spinner would land on during a given number of spins. The spinner has four equal sections. She spun the spinner and recorded the results on the table below.
Based on the table, what is the probability that the spinner will land on the number 5?

Number	Frequency
5	8
7	12
6	11
4	11

Ⓐ 1 out of 8

Ⓑ 4 out of 21

Ⓒ 8 out of 34

Ⓓ 1 out of 4

2. At the Orange County Youth Fair, the number of people attending the weeklong fair is shown on the table. However, the attendance on day 7 was reported incorrectly and was later accurately found to be 12. How does that change the mean of the attendance at the Orange County Youth Fair?

Day	Attendance Each Day (thousands)
1	13
2	15
3	9
4	5
5	16
6	18
7	26

Ⓐ It will decrease by 14,000.

Ⓑ It will decrease by 12,000.

Ⓒ It will decrease by 2,000.

Ⓓ It will increase by 14,000.

Name

1. A teacher asked a group of students to find the mean, median, and mode for the set of numbers below. Which group did it correctly?

12, 8, 16, 12, 13, 19, 16, 77, 15, 10

Ⓐ
Group 1	
Mean	19.8
Mode	12 and 16
Median	14

Ⓑ
Group 2	
Mean	12
Mode	19.8 and 16
Median	14

Ⓒ
Group 3	
Mean	19.8
Mode	12 and 15
Median	16

Ⓓ
Group 4	
Mean	14
Mode	12 and 16
Median	19.8

2. In Mr. Walker's 7th-grade class, the 30 students created a pie chart showing their choices for favorite pet. Based on the class findings, how many students chose cat as their favorite pet?

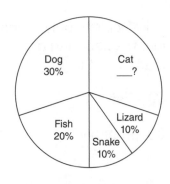

Ⓐ 3

Ⓑ 6

Ⓒ 9

Ⓓ 10

Name

1. Mrs. Mann, a teacher at Roosevelt Junior High, was teaching a lesson on probability. She flipped a coin 100 times. The coin landed on heads 26 times. Based on the results, which of these statements is true?

Ⓐ The coin landed on heads more than expected.

Ⓑ The coin landed on tails less than expected.

Ⓒ The coin landed on tails more than heads.

Ⓓ The coin landed on tails less than heads.

2. Vance has 12 t-shirts hanging in his closet. If 1 out of 4 of these t-shirts are blue, how many blue shirts does Vance have hanging in his closet?

Answer: _____

Name

1. Mrs. Watkins is preparing welcome bags for new teachers at Fanning Elementary. She has pencils in 4 different colors, erasers in 6 different colors, and 2 sizes of pencil sharpeners. If each bag contains one pencil, one eraser, and one sharpener, what is the total number of possible combinations for Mrs. Watkins to place in each bag?

Ⓐ 48   Ⓒ 15

Ⓑ 36   Ⓓ 12

2. Jackson is playing a math board game with his sister. On Jackson's turn, he spins a spinner with five equal sections marked 1, 2, 3, 4, and 5. After he spins, he must roll a 6-sided cube that has one of the following shapes on each side: pentagon, hexagon, square, rectangular prism, circle, and triangle. If Jackson spins a 4 and the cube lands on the triangle, Jackson will win the game. What is the probability that the spinner *and* cube will land on what Jackson needs to win?

Answer: _____

Name

1. For a school newspaper, a student reporter wants to conduct a survey about whether the school football team needs new helmets. Which sampling method will enable the reporter to find the most accurate information?

   (A) Interview all office personnel to find their opinions.

   (B) Interview members of the track team.

   (C) Interview every member of the football team, as well as the coaches and the principal.

   (D) Interview every student who enters the library.

2. Tammy's piggy bank was full of change. She has more pennies than any other coin. She stacked the pennies in piles of different amounts. All together, she created eight stacks of pennies. The number of pennies in each stack is shown below. Which number is the lower quartile for this data set?

   | 35, 26, 28, 30, 32, 49, 36, 50 |

   (A) 26   (B) 29   (C) 23   (D) 31

Name

1. Chandler is helping his mom clean the house. While vacuuming, he takes the cushions off the couch. He finds 7 nickels, 5 dimes, 4 pennies, and 8 quarters. His mom said for him helping her clean, he could have the coins he found. If Chandler puts the coins in his pocket then selects one at random without looking, what is the probability of him selecting a quarter?

   (A) 8 out of 25   (C) 7 out of 24

   (B) 2 out of 5   (D) 1 out of 3

2. Every child that comes to Kendall's birthday party gets a bag with 11 small pieces of gum, 5 medium pieces of gum, and 4 large pieces of gum. If a child selects 1 piece of gum at random, what are the odds of selecting a medium piece of gum?

   (A) 1:4   (C) 1:3

   (B) 3:1   (D) 4:1

1. To study for a multiplication test, Mr. Espinoza divided his class into six groups. Mr. Espinoza would flash a multiplication fact, and the first student to hit a buzzer and answer correctly would earn points for their team. The table shows the number of points earned by each group. What is the mean number of points for the 6 groups?

Groups	Points Earned
Group 1	93
Group 2	70
Group 3	96
Group 4	86
Group 5	91
Group 6	92

Answer: _____

2. A group of students at Taft Junior High surveyed students to find out how early they arrive prior to the start of each school day. Based on the table, which statement is true?

Minutes	# of Students
0–5	IIII
6–10	ⅢⅡ IIII
11–15	I
16–20	II
21–30	IIII

Ⓐ More than half the students arrive at school within 6–10 minutes prior to the start of school.

Ⓑ More than half the students arrive at school more than 15 minutes prior to the start of school.

Ⓒ Half the students come between 6–10 minutes prior to the start of school.

Ⓓ More than half the students arrive at school within 10 minutes prior to the start of school.

1. To prepare a math lesson, a teacher wrote the answer choices on the board before her first-period class arrived. Each student was told to look at the choices and determine which set of data has a range value equal to the median value. If the students answered correctly, which answer choice was given? Round your answer to the nearest hundredth where necessary.

Ⓐ (50, 60, 65, 75, 85)   Ⓒ (12, 18, 20, 23, 24)

Ⓑ (2, 4, 6, 7, 8)   Ⓓ (16, 17, 18, 19, 20)

2. Hannah is learning about mean, median, and mode in her math class. Today, the teacher wrote the following set of numbers on the board. If Hannah did this correctly, what answers did she give?

243, 195, 230, 203, 206, 243, 217

Mean: _____   Median: _____   Mode: _____

Name

1. The scores below show what Hank earned on 8 spelling tests. Which box-and-whisker plot best represents his scores?

78, 73, 81, 73, 93, 62, 79, 69

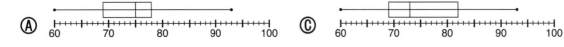

Ⓐ

Ⓒ

Ⓑ

Ⓓ

2. Jennifer asked Garland to find which group of numbers has a range of 21. If Garland did this correctly, which answer choice did he select?

Ⓐ 21, 7, 25, 5, 3

Ⓒ 7, 5, 4, 22, 7

Ⓑ 17, 4, 19, 24, 20

Ⓓ 24, 7, 24, 5, 3

Name

1. The student council at Lincoln Junior High sent home a survey to 305 families to find how many children they have living in their household. How many families have more than 2 but less than 6 children?

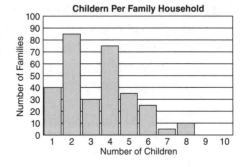

Ⓐ 140 families

Ⓒ 305 families

Ⓑ 250 families

Ⓓ 290 families

2. Match each word with its correct definition.

> **Word Bank**
>
> Mode   Median   Mean

A. _____ is calculated by adding all of the numbers in a set and then dividing the sum by the number of values within the set.

B. _____ is the number in the middle of the set when the numbers are arranged in order from least to greatest.

C. _____ of the set is the number that appears most often within the set.

Name

1. Which statement about an event and a simple event is true?

Ⓐ An event consists of a single outcome, and a simple event is any collection of outcomes in an experiment.

Ⓑ An event consists of multiple outcomes, and a simple event is when there are only 2 outcomes in an experiment.

Ⓒ An event is any collection of outcomes in an experiment, and a simple event consists of a single outcome such as getting heads when flipping a coin.

Ⓓ An event is any collection of single outcomes in a single experiment, and a simple event consists of multiple outcomes.

2. Which statement about a double bar graph is **not** true?

Ⓐ A double bar graph uses vertical bars of different heights to display data.

Ⓑ A double bar graph uses horizontal bars of different heights to display data.

Ⓒ A double bar graph compares two sets of related data for a given value.

Ⓓ A double bar graph shows sets of data by relating how often that data appears in a set of data.

Name

1. A store manager wants to add parking spaces for his store. He decided to graph the number of cars parked in his current lot for a 5-day period. What are the range, mode, median, and mean for this set of data?

Range = _____

Mode = _____

Median = _____

Mean = _____

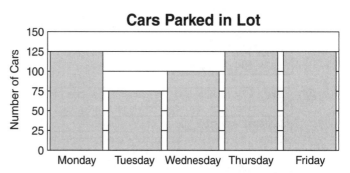

Cars Parked in Lot

2. A teacher created a table with a set of data divided into groups. Which group has a range of 8 and a mean of 10?

Ⓐ Group 1   Ⓒ Group 3

Ⓑ Group 2   Ⓓ Group 4

Group	Data Set
Group 1	6, 9, 9, 15, 10
Group 2	12, 10, 8, 12, 4
Group 3	7, 12, 12, 11, 8
Group 4	13, 6, 14, 9, 8

1. Sam wants to end his school year with an average of 88 in math. So far, he has earned a 93, 85, 73, 88, and 90 on his math tests. For Sam to reach his goal, what score must he earn on his last test to have a mean quiz score of exactly 88?

Ⓐ 100

Ⓒ 95

Ⓑ 99

Ⓓ 88

2. At Junior's Bakery, homemade wheat and white bread is sold by the loaf. The bar graph shows how many loaves of each type were sold during a seven-day period. Is the mean for the number of wheat loaves sold less or greater than that of the white bread?

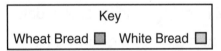

Key	
Wheat Bread ▣	White Bread ▢

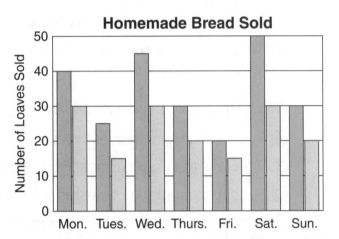

Answer: _____

1. Which table correctly identifies each term?

Ⓐ
Median	the number that falls in the middle when the numbers are listed from least to greatest
Mode	the number that occurs most often
Range	the difference between the greatest and least numbers in the data set
Mean	the sum of the numbers in the data set divided by the number of numbers

Ⓒ
Median	the number that falls in the middle when the numbers are listed from least to greatest
Mode	the number that occurs most often
Mean	the difference between the greatest and least numbers in the data set
Range	the sum of the numbers in the data set divided by the number of numbers

Ⓑ
Mode	the number that falls in the middle when the numbers are listed from least to greatest
Median	the number that occurs most often
Range	the difference between the greatest and least numbers in the data set
Mean	the sum of the numbers in the data set divided by the number of numbers

Ⓓ
Range	the number that falls in the middle when the numbers are listed from least to greatest
Mode	the number that occurs most often
Median	the difference between the greatest and least numbers in the data set
Mean	the sum of the numbers in the data set divided by the number of numbers

2. Mandy is playing a board game with her brother. She needs to roll a cube labeled with numbers 1 through 6. If the cube lands on an even number on her next three attempts, she wins the game. On her first roll, the cube lands on 4. On her second roll, the cube lands on 2. What is the probability that the cube will land on an even number on her third roll, therefore allowing Mandy to win the game?

Ⓐ 4 out of 6   Ⓑ 1 out of 2   Ⓒ 1 out of 6   Ⓓ 1 out of 3

Name

1. Melvin flipped a coin three times in his math class. Which table lists all the possible combinations he could have flipped?

Ⓐ
1st Flip	2nd Flip	3rd Flip	Results
H	H	H	HHH
H	H	T	HHT
T	T	T	TTT
H	T	H	HTH

Ⓑ
1st Flip	2nd Flip	3rd Flip	Results
H	H	H	HHH
H	H	T	HHT
T	T	T	TTT
H	T	H	HTH
T	T	H	TTH
H	T	T	HTT
T	H	T	THT

Ⓒ
1st Flip	2nd Flip	3rd Flip	Results
H	H	H	HHH
H	H	T	HHT
T	T	T	TTT
H	T	H	HTH
T	T	H	TTH
H	T	T	HTT
T	H	T	THT
T	H	H	THH

Ⓓ
1st Flip	2nd Flip	3rd Flip	Results
H	H	H	HHH
H	H	T	HHT
T	T	T	TTT
H	T	H	HTH
T	T	H	TTH
H	T	T	HTT
T	H	T	THT

2. Marsha created the table below to show the number of birds she saw in a span of 7 days. Which measure of the data represents the difference between the greatest and least number of birds seen?

Ⓐ Median

Ⓒ Mean

Ⓑ Mode

Ⓓ Range

Day	Number of Birds Seen
1	67
2	12
3	78
4	9
5	72
6	19
7	69

Name

1. Mary took the temperature outside during a 7-day period. Based on the data, what is the closest mean for the set of temperatures Mary took?

Ⓐ 88.7°F

Ⓒ 87.4°F

Ⓑ 87.1°F

Ⓓ 86.7°F

7 Day Temperatures		
88°F	92°F	89°F
90°F	90°F	83°F
78°F		

2. The data set below consists of the scores students in Mr. Rowland's math class earned on a test. Which stem-and-leaf plot shows this data correctly?

96, 68, 71, 70, 88, 79, 74, 74, 81, 92, 83, 86, 81, 88, 90, 81, 91, 93, 96, 62

Ⓐ
```
6 | 2 8 8
7 | 0 1 4 4 9
8 | 1 1 1 3 6 8
9 | 0 2 3 3 6
```

Ⓑ
```
6 | 2 8
7 | 0 1 4 4 9
8 | 1 1 1 3 6 8
9 | 0 2 3 3 6 6
```

Ⓒ
```
6 | 2 8
7 | 9 1 4 4
8 | 1 1 1 3 6 8 8
9 | 0 2 3 3 6 6
```

Ⓓ
```
6 | 2 8
7 | 0 1 4 4 9
8 | 1 1 1 3 6 8 8
9 | 0 1 2 3 6 6
```

Name

1. Mandy was asked by her manager to create a table showing the number of customers that come into their store from opening at 10:00 a.m. until 12:00 p.m. for a 12-day period. Which days represent outliers for the data set?

Day	1	2	3	4	5	6	7	8	9	10	11	12
# of Customers	46	40	39	3	54	43	38	5	49	45	49	51

Ⓐ Day 5 and Day 12

Ⓒ Day 3 and Day 7

Ⓑ Day 4 and Day 8

Ⓓ Day 9 and Day 11

2. Mrs. Brooks divided her students into two teams for a math game. The table shows the scores both teams scored in 5 rounds. The goal is to have the highest mean score. Which team won, and what was their mean score rounded to the nearest whole number?

Team Renegades	Team Tough
44	46
38	32
38	56
67	31
46	39

Ⓐ Team Tough: 39

Ⓒ Team Renegades: 47

Ⓑ Team Renegades: 41

Ⓓ Team Tough: 47

Name

1. Over a 2-day period, a manager at Harry's Café surveyed 200 customers to find out their favorite food. The results are shown in the table. Which of the following statements supports data from the survey?

Ⓐ The median of the data is 30.

Ⓑ 60% of the customers prefer grilled ham & cheese.

Ⓒ Grilled ham & cheese and hamburger pizza were the favorites of half of the customers surveyed.

Ⓓ Fried chicken takes too long to cook, and therefore, nobody ordered it.

Favorite Food	Number of Customers
Grilled Ham & Cheese	60
Burgers	30
Hamburger Pizza	40
Chicken Tenders	20
Fried Chicken	10
Chicken Fried Steak	20
Fried Salmon Patties	20

2. Summer has 7 quarters, 4 nickels, 3 pennies, and 7 dimes in her pocket. If she reaches in without looking, what is the probability she will select a dime?

Ⓐ 1 out of 7 chance

Ⓒ 4 out of 21 chance

Ⓑ 1 out of 3 chance

Ⓓ 7 out of 20 chance

Name

1. Michael has a new kite. He recorded how high he flew the kite over a 5-day period. Which statement is *not* supported by the graph?

Ⓐ Wednesday and Friday's heights added together is the same as Monday, Tuesday, and Thursday.

Ⓑ Michael flew the kite 75 feet higher each day than the day before.

Ⓒ Tuesday and Wednesday's heights added together is the same as Friday's height.

Ⓓ The median height flown is 225 ft.

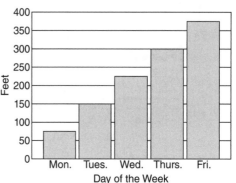

2. A coach asked 8 boys to divide into teams of two to practice throwing and catching during physical education. The boys' names are Sam, Fred, Luke, Jorge, Henry, David, Billy, and Carl. How many possible combinations of teams of 2 can the boys create?

Answer: _____

Name

1. Sandra looked at several different sized vases to purchase for her dining table. She planned on putting different flowers in the vase each month. The vases varied in price from $32.75 to $41.45, and she finally settled on the one she wanted. Which measure of data can be used to describe the variation in price of the vases?

Ⓐ mean   Ⓑ range   Ⓒ mode   Ⓓ median

2. Mr. Anglin teaches 4 classes of algebra at VanBuren High School. He conducted a survey to find which students plan on applying to junior colleges and 4-year colleges. The results of the survey are listed. Which Venn diagram best presents Mr. Anglin's findings?

- A total of 40 students plan to send applications to junior colleges.

- A total of 80 students plan to apply to 4-year colleges.

- 20 of the students surveyed plan to send applications to both junior and 4-year colleges.

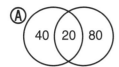   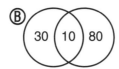   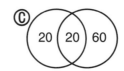   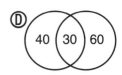

Name

1. At Smokey Joe's BBQ, when a customer orders the brisket plate, they get a choice of 3 side dishes. The side dishes are banana pudding, cole slaw, beans, or potato salad. Which list shows all the possible combinations of 3 different side dishes a customer can choose from?

Ⓐ
- banana pudding, beans, and cole slaw
- banana pudding, beans, and potato salad
- banana pudding, cole slaw, and potato salad
- beans, cole slaw, and potato salad

Ⓒ
- banana pudding, beans, and cole slaw
- banana pudding, beans, and potato salad
- banana pudding, cole slaw, and potato salad
- potato salad, cole slaw, and potato salad

Ⓑ
- banana pudding, beans, and cole slaw
- banana pudding, beans, and beans
- banana pudding, cole slaw, and potato salad
- beans, cole slaw, and potato salad

Ⓓ
- banana pudding, beans, and cole slaw
- banana pudding, beans, and potato salad

2. Marcus recorded the color of cars parked in a parking lot. So far, he has counted 250 cars in the lot. Based on the data, what is the probability that the next car to pull into the lot will be white or green?

Color	# of Cars
White	50
Red	30
Yellow	20
Blue	80
Green	70

Answer: _____

Name

1. The table shows the number of points two twin brothers scored in the first 5 basketball games of the season. What is the difference between the median number of points Luke scored and the median number of points Larry scored?

Larry	9	8	16	13	15
Luke	11	6	7	8	12

Answer: _____

2. Chandler went fishing at his Uncle Lawrence's pond. He caught 2 bass, 3 yellow catfish, 5 blue catfish, and 10 perch. After fishing, Chandler decided he wanted to give his uncle a fish. If he chooses one fish at random, what is the probability that it is a yellow catfish?

Ⓐ 3 out of 4

Ⓑ 3 out of 20

Ⓒ 1 out of 4

Ⓓ 1 out of 2

1. Wanda is making a flower garden in her back yard. The garden is going to be either round, rectangular, or oval. It will be 5 feet, 8 feet, or 12 feet in length. She will plant one of the following colors of hibiscus in the garden: blue, green, pink, or white. How many different garden combinations does Wanda have to choose from?

Answer: _____

2. The table shows the number of students absent at Madison Junior High in three grade levels during a three-month period. Which bar graph represents the data correctly.

Month	6th Grade	7th Grade	8th Grade
January	20	18	25
February	16	12	19
March	12	9	7

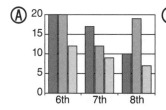 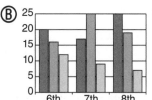 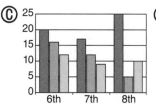 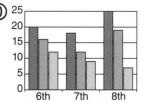

1. Lee has a giant gumball machine. Inside, he has 34 red gumballs, 27 blue gumballs, and 14 white gumballs. If Lee places a quarter in the machine, what is the probability that Lee will get a white gumball? Round your answer to the nearest whole percent.

Ⓐ 45% Ⓒ 19%

Ⓑ 36% Ⓓ not given

2. Mrs. Anderson is teaching her students about range, mean, mode, and median. She wrote the numbers below on the board. She then asked her students to find which number affects the range of the numbers more than the others. If her students did this correctly, which number did they give?

37, 29, 12, 25, 25, 32, 31

Ⓐ 32 Ⓒ 25

Ⓑ 29 Ⓓ 12

Name

1. The information below is compiled from a survey of 40 students in Mr. Roddy's social-studies class. Use the information to complete the Venn diagram.

   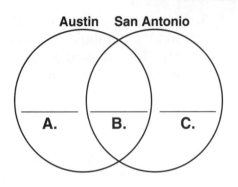

   - A total of 20 students have been to Austin, Texas.
   - A total of 35 students have been to San Antonio, Texas.
   - 15 of the students have been to both Austin and San Antonio, Texas.

2. Which statement about independent and dependent events is true?

   Ⓐ A dependent event is one in which the outcome of the second event is influenced by the outcome of the first event. If events are independent, when one event happens, it doesn't affect the outcome of the next event.

   Ⓑ A dependent and independent event both influence the second event, not the first.

   Ⓒ A dependent event is one in which the outcome of the second event is influenced by the outcome of the first event. For an event to be independent, there must be a dependent event.

   Ⓓ A dependent event solely rests on the outcome of an independent event.

Name

1. A manager at Sunny's Diner wants to graph the number of parked cars in the parking lot to determine a trend for peak store times during a 7-day period. Based on this information, which of the following is the best type of graph to accomplish this task?

   Ⓐ stem-and-leaf plot

   Ⓒ circle graph

   Ⓑ line graph

   Ⓓ pictograph

2. Explain what **probability** means.

   _____

   _____

   _____

1. Three friends created a table comparing their grades on five assignments. Which statement below is true about the mean for this data set?

Ⓐ mean of student 1 > mean of student 2

Ⓑ mean of student 3 = mean of student 1

Ⓒ mean of student 1 < mean of student 3

Ⓓ mean of student 2 = mean of student 1

Student	Grades
1	82, 77, 80, 75, 100
2	85, 84, 92, 89, 82
3	90, 88, 79, 85, 80

2. Mark likes making survivor bracelets out of paracord. Yesterday, he purchased 6 tiles marked *G, E, A, O, T*, and *H* to use on his bracelets. The letter tiles are in a package. If Mark reaches in and selects one tile at random, what is the probability he will select a tile that has a vowel printed on it?

Ⓐ 1 out of 6

Ⓑ 2 out of 3

Ⓒ 1 out of 3

Ⓓ 1 out of 2

1. Andrew is making dessert for his father. The table shows the different choices that Andrew has at his house for making an ice-cream treat. Andrew will randomly select one flavor, one topping, and one fruit for his father. What is the probability that he will make a dessert with vanilla, blueberries, and whipped cream?

Ice Cream Flavor	Fruit	Toppings
Strawberry	Blueberry	Whipped Cream
Chocolate	Banana	Granola
Vanilla		

Ⓐ 3 out of 7   Ⓑ 3 out of 12   Ⓒ 1 out of 6   Ⓓ 1 out of 12

2. Jennifer forgot the combination to her locker at school. She knows the numbers are 4, 9, 2, and 6, but she can't remember the order. How many possible combinations can there be to Jennifer's locker using these numbers without repeating?

Answer: _____

Name

1. The seventh-grade student council at Franklin Junior High was asked to collect data to find suggestions on what color to paint the 7th-grade hallway. Which group should the student council survey to collect the most reliable data?

   Ⓐ All 8th-grade students.

   Ⓑ Every student who enters the library.

   Ⓒ Random 7th-grade students from each 7th-grade classroom.

   Ⓓ All students that play sports, including cheerleaders.

2. The plot below shows the ages of neighborhood volunteers who pick up trash in a vacant lot. Which of the following is true according to the data on the plot?

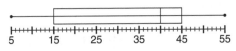

   Ⓐ median = 40

   Ⓒ median = 30

   Ⓑ mean = 30

   Ⓓ mean = 40

Name

1. An attendance clerk at Lexington Junior High recorded the number of students tardy for 2nd-period classes during the first ten days of every month in the school year. She recorded her findings as shown in the table. She then found the minimum, median, and maximum of the data set. Which answer choice shows her findings?

   Ⓐ 5, 12, 25

   Ⓑ 5, 13, 25

   Ⓒ 8, 12, 22

   Ⓓ 8, 13, 22

September - 22	October - 10
November - 5	December - 8
January - 15	February - 11
March - 25	April - 17
May - 13	June - 8

2. Referring to the data above, what would the attendance clerk get if she subtracted the minimum number from the maximum number of the data set?

   Ⓐ mode

   Ⓒ median

   Ⓑ mean

   Ⓓ range

1. A teacher asked her students to think of a math term and definition. She then asked Sam, a student in the class, to come to the board and write his definition on the board but not the term it defines. She asked the students to fill in the missing term. The answer choices below are the answers the class gave to the problem. Which answer choice is correct?

Ⓐ bar graph

Ⓒ stem-and-leaf plot

Ⓑ circle graph

Ⓓ box-and-whisker

Sam's Problem

_____ is an arrangement of numbers that separates the digits into columns of place value.

2. On a graph, what is the counting method used to label an axis?

Ⓐ key

Ⓒ horizontal axis

Ⓑ scale

Ⓓ vertical axis

1. Michael wants to use a graph to compare and contrast two or three categories of two animals he is researching for his science project. Which answer choice below is the best way to do so?

Ⓐ circle graph

Ⓒ line graph

Ⓑ pictograph

Ⓓ Venn diagram

2. If you want to graph change over time, which method would be the best way to present the data?

Ⓐ line graph

Ⓒ circle graph

Ⓑ pictograph

Ⓓ bar graph

Name

1. Which answer choice is the best definition of **probability**?

   Ⓐ the likeliness of something happening more than once

   Ⓑ the ratio of only favorable outcomes

   Ⓒ the ratio of unfavorable outcomes

   Ⓓ the ratio of favorable outcomes to possible outcomes

2. Which answer choice below defines two or more events in which the outcome of one event does not affect the outcome of the other event?

   Ⓐ simple probability

   Ⓑ dependent events

   Ⓒ independent events

   Ⓓ fluke events

Name

1. What are possible end results to an experiment called?

   Ⓐ winning   Ⓒ outcomes

   Ⓑ losing   Ⓓ probability

2. Matt and his friends collect marbles. Frequently, they trade marbles after school. The table shows the most popular colors and how many Matt has traded so far. Considering the data, how many of the next 6 trades Matt does should he expect to be for a blue marble?

   Ⓐ 2   Ⓒ 5

   Ⓑ 4   Ⓓ 6

Marbles Traded	
Blue	5
Brown	2
White	1
Red	7

Name

1. Mrs. Norquist's 7th-grade math class is having a bake sale as a fundraiser for new calculators. The first day, they sold 16 donuts. Of these donuts, 4 were glazed. Considering the data, how many of the next 8 donuts would you expect to be glazed?

Ⓐ 4

Ⓒ 2

Ⓑ 3

Ⓓ 1

2. Gordon is playing a game with his sister Brandi. The spinner they used for the game is shown below. If Gordon spins the spinner 9 times, which answer choice is the best prediction of how many times it will land on 2?

Ⓐ 3

Ⓒ 5

Ⓑ 4

Ⓓ 6

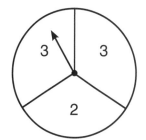

Name

1. Chase conducted a survey to find the number of students at Ford Junior High to find the number of students who were part of the swim team, track team, basketball team, or a combination of all. The Venn diagram below shows the results. What is the total number of students who are part of the swim team and/or track team but not the basketball team?

Ⓐ 18 students

Ⓒ 80 students

Ⓑ 94 students

Ⓓ 10 students

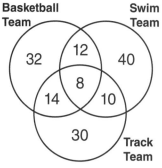

2. Margo is scanning for music on her stereo. Each time she hits the scan button, a different genre of music plays. She records what she hears in the table. Considering the data, how many of the next 20 scans would you expect to be country?

Ⓐ 1

Ⓒ 3

Ⓑ 2

Ⓓ 4

Type	# of Songs
Rock	13
Country	2
Pop	4
Jazz	1

Name

1. Ella, Izzie, and Andrew are competing for 1st, 2nd, and 3rd place in a 400-meter freestyle swim. Complete the table by showing all the possible outcomes for the race.

1st Place	2nd Place	3rd Place

2. For Terri's birthday, she went on a shopping spree. She purchased 2 pairs of shoes, 4 shirts, and 2 pairs of pants. How many wardrobe combinations will Terri have?

Answer: _____

Name

1. Henry bought a new lock for his locker at school. For the combination on his last lock, he used a 3-digit number but forgot it and had to have the lock cut off. This time, he decided to create a two-digit combination using the numbers 1, 2, 5, 7, and 9. How many different two-digit numbers can Henry make? Hint: Numbers can be repeated.

Answer: _____

2. Coach Anglin created this stem-and-leaf plot to show the total number of points scored by each of his 24 players on the 7th-grade basketball team over the course of the season. Based on this information, what fraction of the players scored more than 65 points during the season?

Ⓐ $\frac{5}{24}$ Ⓒ $\frac{1}{4}$

Ⓑ $\frac{3}{4}$ Ⓓ $\frac{7}{24}$

Points Scored by Basketball Team

2	8 9
4	1 2 5 5 9
5	1 2 2 4 5 8 9 9
6	2 4 4 7
7	0 2 5
8	3 8

Name

1. For each multiplication contest, points were awarded by the teacher to winning students. At the end of the year, the top ten scores were awarded prizes. These scores are shown below. Which stem-and-leaf plot correctly represents these scores?

| 385 | 400 | 379 | 388 | 359 |
| 388 | 350 | 398 | 355 | 388 |

Ⓐ
```
35 | 0  5  9
37 | 9
38 | 5  8
39 | 8
40 |
```

Ⓑ
```
35 | 0  5  9
37 | 9
38 | 5  8  8
39 | 8  9
40 | 0
```

Ⓒ
```
35 | 0  5  9
37 | 9
38 | 5  8  8  8
39 | 8
40 | 0
```

Ⓓ
```
35 | 0  5  9
37 | 9
38 | 5  8
39 | 8
40 |
```

2. Samantha scored 70 on two of her first math tests. She then scored 65, 80, and 85. What is her average (mean) score in math?

Answer: _____

Name

1. Pete is playing a game in which he has to spin a colored spinner and roll a die (numbered 1–6) to determine which color route he takes on the game board and how many moves forward he gets to advance. On his next turn, Pete will win the game if he does not land on blue and the die does not land on 5. What is the probability that Pete will win on his next turn?

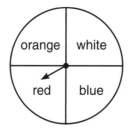
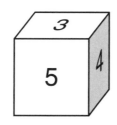

Answer: _____

2. A teacher was teaching his students about probability. He asked a student to come to his desk and roll two standard dice to find their sum. When Mark was called, his teacher asked him what the probability of him rolling a sum of seven would be. If Mark answered the question correctly, which answer choice below did Mark give?

Ⓐ $\frac{9}{36}$

Ⓒ $\frac{1}{6}$

Ⓑ $\frac{6}{30}$

Ⓓ $\frac{1}{2}$

1. Hank rolled a pair of dice and got a sum of 8. He then rolled a pair of dice again and got a sum of 2. He rolled a third time and got a sum of 3. He asked his friend how many total outcomes are possible when rolling a pair of dice. He then asked how many total outcomes are possible for rolling a sum of 3.

There are _____ possible outcomes when rolling a pair of dice.

There are _____ ways of getting a sum of three when rolling two dice.

2. Look at the numbers below. Create a box-and-whisker plot above the number line to represent the data. What is the median of the data?

> **19, 5, 9, 8, 16, 12, 15**

Ⓐ 16   Ⓒ 8

Ⓑ 12   Ⓓ 5

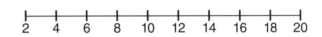

2 4 6 8 10 12 14 16 18 20

---

1. Susan is playing a board game. She needs to spin a 5, 6, or 7 to win. Which of the answer choices below best describes Susan's chances of landing on one of these numbers in one spin?

Ⓐ likely   Ⓒ unlikely

Ⓑ certain   Ⓓ guaranteed

2. The numbers below represent the amount of people who visited the wetlands for a 10-day period. Using the data collected, calculate the following statistics.

> **31 76 91 22 76 89 57 59 43 54**

Range: _____   Mean: _____

Median: _____   Mode: _____

Name

1. Where Melissa works, the refrigerator is always full of beverages. The table shows the outcomes for Melissa's first 60 times visiting the refrigerator to randomly select a drink. In Melissa's next 40 visits to the refrigerator, how many times will she randomly select tea as her drink of choice?

Drink Choice	
Water	22
Root Beer	8
Cola	20
Tea	3
Strawberry Punch	4
Coffee	3

Ⓐ 6

Ⓒ 4

Ⓑ 5

Ⓓ 2

2. Lee loves sports cars. The data below shows the prices, in thousands of dollars, of 15 sports cars Lee would love to purchase. What is the median price, in thousands of dollars, of these sports cars?

63K 75K 85K 65K 77K 91K 25K 65K 81K 51K 69K 82K 52K 72K 83K

Ⓐ 75K dollars

Ⓑ 69K dollars

Ⓒ 72K dollars

Ⓓ 65K dollars

Name

1. Lex scored 77, 84, 68, 98, and 89. What two scores must Lex earn on his next 2 tests to have an overall mean of 85?

Ⓐ 84 and 89

Ⓑ 85 and 85

Ⓒ 86 and 80

Ⓓ 87 and 92

2. What is the best definition of a line plot?

Ⓐ a graph with bars showing related data

Ⓑ a graph showing the frequency of data on a number line

Ⓒ a graph in the shape of a circle showing related data

Ⓓ a graph identical to a stem-and-leaf plot

1. What is the best description of what a double bar graph is used for?

Ⓐ It's a single bar graph showing one set of data.

Ⓑ It's a single bar graph showing two sets of data.

Ⓒ To show two sets of data presented in a bar graph formation for the purpose of comparison.

Ⓓ It's used only for decoration purposes.

2. Why is a tree diagram used for combination problems?

Ⓐ A tree diagram represents all possible outcomes of a probability experiment.

Ⓑ A tree diagram represents all unlikely outcomes of probability experiment.

Ⓒ A tree diagram only lists likely combinations.

Ⓓ A tree diagram only lists favorable combinations or outcomes.

1. Michelle and Dave bought a box of pens. Inside, there were 4 blue pens and 6 black pens. Michelle randomly picked a pen from the box and kept it. Then, Dave did the same. What is the probability Michelle and Dave will both pick a black pen?

Ⓐ $\frac{1}{36}$ Ⓒ $\frac{9}{25}$

Ⓑ $\frac{1}{30}$ Ⓓ $\frac{1}{3}$

2. The bar graph shows the number of canned goods donated to charity by either boys, girls, or adults at Kennedy Junior High. Based on the graph, which statement must be true?

Ⓐ Teachers donated more canned goods than boys and girls combined.

Ⓑ Boys donated more than any group.

Ⓒ Girls and boys donated more than adults.

Ⓓ Adults donated twice as much as boys.

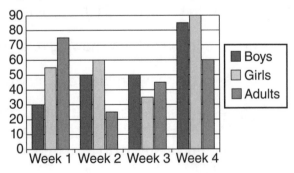

1. Gunther is playing a game. He spins a spinner with 5 equal sections labeled orange, blue, yellow, green, and pink. Then, he rolls a cube numbered 1 through 6. What is the probability that the arrow will stop on the color orange and the cube will land on the number 2?

   Ⓐ $\frac{1}{5}$ Ⓒ $\frac{1}{11}$

   Ⓑ $\frac{1}{6}$ Ⓓ $\frac{1}{30}$

2. Jimmy plays on the varsity basketball team. Based on the coach's basketball statistics, one out of four of Jimmy's shots makes it into the basket. If Jimmy takes 20 shots during the next game, how many baskets will Jimmy most likely score?

   Ⓐ 20

   Ⓑ 10

   Ⓒ 5

   Ⓓ 2

1. Mrs. Ganske wants to conduct a survey about whether new computers should be added to the Eisenhower Junior High computer lab. Which sampling method will offer Mrs. Ganske the best results?

   Ⓐ Interview every 3rd student who enters the computer lab.

   Ⓑ Interview every 20th student on the campus roster as well as teachers.

   Ⓒ Interview all students on the football team.

   Ⓓ Interview all students who ride the bus to school.

2. Susan found 1 quarter, 1 dime, and 1 nickel in her dad's truck. She decides to play heads or tails with all three coins. If she tosses all the coins in the air at the same time, how many possible outcomes are there?

Answer: _____

Name

1. At Donny's Diner, a customer can choose from meatloaf, chicken, or spaghetti. They can have water, cola, or tea. How many different combinations of one meal and one drink can a customer choose from?

Answer: _____

2. Peter wants to buy a new shirt to wear for a birthday party. He found a shirt he likes. The shirt comes in green, blue, black, red, or gray. The sizes available are small, medium, or large. The shirt is available in cotton or silk. How many different combinations of material, color, and size are possible for Peter to choose from?

Answer: _____

Name

1. Terry is playing a game. If she picks a card from below and rolls a standard die, how many total outcomes are possible?

Ⓐ 6

Ⓑ 12

Ⓒ 18

Ⓓ 24

| Green | Red | Blue |

2. Gerald has a deck of 20 cards numbered 1–20. All the cards were thrown into a basket. What is the probability he draws an even-numbered card that is less than 15?

Answer: _____

Warm-Up 1
1. C   2. 65

Warm-Up 2
1. C   2. A

Warm-Up 3
1. D   2. C

Warm-Up 4
1. B   2. 6 uniforms

Warm-Up 5
1. D   2. C

Warm-Up 6
1. A   2. 12 combinations

Warm-Up 7
1. B   2. 24 outfits

Warm-Up 8
1. D   2. C

Warm-Up 9
1. $\frac{1}{2}$ lb.; $2\frac{1}{2}$ lbs.   2. Ella = 21 pt. average
                          Libby = 23 pt. average

Warm-Up 10
1. A   2. 94

Warm-Up 11
1. $\frac{7}{15}$ 2. A

Warm-Up 12
1. B   2. C

Warm-Up 13
1. B   2. C

Warm-Up 14
1. A   2. C

Warm-Up 15
1. C   2. 3 blue shirts

Warm-Up 16
1. A   2. 1 out of 30

Warm-Up 17
1. C   2. B

Warm-Up 18
1. D   2. C

Warm-Up 19
1. 88.33   2. D

Warm-Up 20
1. B   2. Mean = 219.57
              Median = 217
              Mode = 243

Warm-Up 21
1. D   2. D

Warm-Up 22
1. A   2. **A.** Mean; **B.** Median; **C.** Mode

Warm-Up 23
1. C   2. D

Warm-Up 24
1. Range = 50   2. D
   Mode = 125
   Median = 125
   Mean = 110

Warm-Up 25
1. B   2. greater

Warm-Up 26
1. A   2. B

Warm-Up 27
1. C   2. D

Warm-Up 28
1. B   2. D

Warm-Up 29
1. B   2. C

Warm-Up 30
1. C   2. B

Warm-Up 31
1. A   2. 28 combinations

Warm-Up 32
1. B   2. C

Warm-Up 33
1. A   2. 12 out of 25

Warm-Up 34
1. 5 points   2. B

Warm-Up 35
1. 36 combinations 2. D

Warm-Up 36
1. C   2. D

Warm-Up 37

1.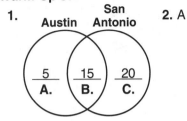

2. A

Warm-Up 38

1. B

2. Probability is how likely it is that something will happen based on the possible outcomes.

Warm-Up 39

1. C

2. D

Warm-Up 40

1. D

2. 24 combinations

Warm-Up 41

1. C

2. A

Warm-Up 42

1. A

2. D

Warm-Up 43

1. C

2. B

Warm-Up 44

1. D

2. A

Warm-Up 45

1. D

2. C

Warm-Up 46

1. C

2. A

Warm-Up 47

1. C

2. A

Warm-Up 48

1. C

2. B

Warm-Up 49

1.

1st Place	2nd Place	3rd Place
Ella	Izzie	Andrew
Ella	Andrew	Izzie
Izzie	Ella	Andrew
Izzie	Andrew	Ella
Andrew	Izzie	Ella
Andrew	Ella	Izzie

2. 16 combinations

Warm-Up 50

1. 25 different combinations

2. C

Warm-Up 51

1. C

2. 74

Warm-Up 52

1. 5 out of 8

2. C

Warm-Up 53

1. 36 and 2

2. B;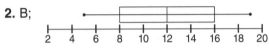

Warm-Up 54

1. C

2. Range: 69   Mean: 59.8
   Median: 58.0   Mode: 76

Warm-Up 55

1. D

2. C

Warm-Up 56

1. D

2. B

Warm-Up 57

1. C

2. A

Warm-Up 58

1. D

2. C

Warm-Up 59

1. D

2. C

Warm-Up 60

1. B

2. 8 possible outcomes

Warm-Up 61

1. 9 combinations

2. 30 combinations

Warm-Up 62

1. C

2. $\frac{7}{20}$

Algebra
Patterns
Functions

Name _____

1. Kristi and David are walking on the beach collecting seashells. David found 12 more than twice the number of seashells that Kristi had collected. If k stands for the number of seashells Kristi found, and d stands for the number of seashells David found, which equation could be used to find how many seashells David found?

Ⓐ $d = 2k \times 12$ Ⓒ $k = 2d \times 12$

Ⓑ $d = 2k + 12$ Ⓓ $k = (2d + 12) - d$

2. At Washington Junior High, 75% of the 600 students buy hot lunch at school. How many students buy hot lunch?

Answer: _____

Name _____

1. Jennifer is buying her daughters new backpacks for school. The cost of backpacks runs from $10 to $40. All backpacks marked $20 or higher are 30% off regular price. Jennifer bought 1 backpack marked $20 and a second backpack marked $40. What is the price Jennifer will pay for both backpacks before tax?

Answer: _____

2. The sum of a number (n) and 14 is 72. Which equation shows this relationship?

Ⓐ $72 + n = 14$ Ⓒ $14 - n - 72$

Ⓑ $14 + n = 72$ Ⓓ $72n = 14$

Name

1. Jerry wants to buy a new video game. The video game costs $60. So far, Jerry has $32. He can earn $5 an hour raking leaves from his neighbors' lawns. Using the equation below, how many hours must Jerry work in order to earn the money he needs?

   Ⓐ 5 hours   Ⓒ 3 hours

   Ⓑ 4 hours   Ⓓ 6 hours

> $5h + 32 = 60$
>
> $x =$ _____

2. A teacher told his students he was thinking of a number. He said that the sum of the number (n) and 36 is 89. He then asked his students to figure out which equation below best describes this relationship. If his students answered correctly, what answer did they give? Solve for n.

   Ⓐ $89 + n = 36$ Ⓒ $89n = 36$

   Ⓑ $36 - n = 89$ Ⓓ $36 + n = 89$

                                    $n =$ _____

Name

1. The price for admission to a water park is $12. Which of the following expressions can be used to represent the price of admission for a certain number of tickets.

   Ⓐ $12 + t$

   Ⓑ $12 - t$

   Ⓒ $12 \times t$

   Ⓓ $12 \div t$

2. Sophia wrote the equation in the box. What is the solution to the equation Sophia wrote? Show your work.

> **Sophia's Equation**
>
> $x + 7 = -11$
>
> $x =$ _____

1. Mitchell wrote the expression shown on the board. Simplify the expression and choose the best answer.

   (A) -5x

   (B) 5x – 12

   (C) -5x – 12

   (D) 8x – 3x – 12

   > $8x + 8 - 20 - 3x$

2. Calculate the value of x for the equation in the box. Show your work.

   (A) 2

   (B) 4

   (C) 6

   (D) 8

   > $3x + 3x = 20 - 8$
   >
   > X = _____

1. Russell loves wearing bow ties. He has collected 12. If 2 out of every 3 bow ties are black with different colored stripes, how many black bow ties with different colored stripes does Russell own?

   Answer: _____

2. Cody wrote the equation below. He asked Gordon to find the value of n. If Gordon did this correctly, which answer below did he give?

   (A) 13

   (B) 12

   (C) 11

   (D) 10

   > $2n + 1 = 21$

Name _____

1. Patricia is trying to solve the equation in the box. Which answer below is the value of *x* that makes the equation true?

(A) 5

(B) 7

(C) 8

(D) 9

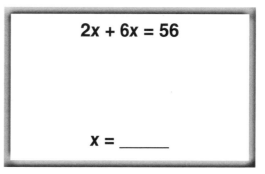

$$2x + 6x = 56$$

X = _____

2. Russell went to a book store where used books are sold. He plans to buy mystery books that cost $7 each. Russell has $25 to spend but wants to save $4 for a hamburger and fries. How many books can Russell purchase?

(A) 5 books

(B) 4 books

(C) 3 books

(D) 2 books

Name _____

1. For a fundraiser, tickets are being sold for $62 each to aid tornado victims. Complete the table to show the amount of money raised. If *x* represents the number of tickets sold, which equation represents the data in the table?

(A) $\frac{62}{x}$

(B) $62x + 8$

(C) $62x - 8$

(D) $62x$

Tickets Sold	Money Raised
4	$
7	$
10	$
15	$

2. Mrs. Harrison is a librarian at Country Hills Elementary. At the end of each day, she returns books back to the shelves to get ready for the next day. The table shows the amount of time it takes her to reshelve books based on the number of books that were returned. Complete the table based on the function $y = x + 6$. What do *x* and *y* represent?

x = _____

y = _____

x	y
5	11
25	
35	
	51

Name

1. When Robbie arrived at his classroom, this expression was written on a sheet of paper sitting on his desk as a math warm-up. Help Robbie simplify the expression.

$$2(a + 4) + 7(4a - 6)$$

2. Marty thought of a number. He told his friend that six less than a number is 17. If Marty's friend wrote an equation to find Marty's missing number, which equation below will give the missing number? Solve for n.

Ⓐ $6 - n = 17$

Ⓒ $17 + 6 = n$

Ⓑ $n - 17 = 6$

Ⓓ $n - 6 = 17$

$n = $ _____

Name

1. John is trying to figure out the rule for the ordered pairs in the table below. If his older brother helps him find the correct answer, which answer identifies the rule used in the table?

Ⓐ $y = 3x - 1$

Ⓒ $y = 2x + 1$

Ⓑ $y = 3x + 2$

Ⓓ $y = 2x - 1$

x	y
1	1
2	3
3	5
4	7

2. Jeff was asked to simplify the problem in the box. Help Jeff simplify the expression.

$$6(a - 2b) + 3(4a + b)$$

Name

1. Hannah is playing an ordered-pair game with her mom. The card she drew asked which ordered pair (x, y) makes the equation $y = x + 4$ true? If Hannah answered correctly, which answer choice did Hannah select?

Ⓐ (2, 4)

Ⓒ (6, 4)

Ⓑ (2, 6)

Ⓓ (3, 0)

2. Four groups of students were asked to find sets of ordered pairs that satisfy $y = 2x + 3$. Which group did this correctly?

Ⓐ Group 1

Ⓒ Group 3

Ⓑ Group 2

Ⓓ Group 4

Group	Ordered Pairs
Group 1	(0, 2) (1, 3) (2, 4)
Group 2	(0, 2) (1, 5) (2, 8)
Group 3	(0, 3) (1, 4) (2, 5)
Group 4	(0, 3) (1, 5) (2, 7)

Name

1. Which student solved the two equations correctly?

Ⓐ Roman: Question 1 is $y = 1$, and Question 2 is $x = 2$

Ⓑ Marta: Question 1 is $y = 2$, and Question 2 is $x = 4$

Ⓒ Louis: Question 1 is $y = 4$, and Question 2 is $x = 2$

Ⓓ Sarah: Question 1 is $y = 2$, and Question 2 is $x = 2$

Question	Equation
1	$6 - 2y = 2$
2	$8 = 3x + 2$

2. Find the value for the expression using the terms $x = 5$ and $y = 2$.

$$\frac{1}{2}y - x$$

Ⓐ -1

Ⓒ -4

Ⓑ -6

Ⓓ -3

Name

1. Four groups of students were asked to write an expression that has a value of -3. Which group did this correctly?

Ⓐ	Ⓑ	Ⓒ	Ⓓ
Group 1	**Group 2**	**Group 3**	**Group 4**
$-4 - (7)$	$-7 - (-4)$	$-4 - (-7)$	$-7 - (4)$

2. A teacher asked four students what rule identifies the sequence of numbers shown below. Circle which student answered correctly.

1, -3, 9, -27

Jake – Multiply the preceding number by 3.

Edward – Divide the preceding number by 3.

Bella – Multiply the preceding number by -3.

Atto – Divide the preceding number by -3.

Name

1. A teacher wrote the equation $y = 2x + 1$ on the board in her classroom. She divided her class into groups of four to create a table based on her equation. Which group did this correctly?

Ⓐ
x	y
0	1
1	3
2	5
3	7
4	9
5	11

Ⓑ
x	y
-2	5
-1	3
0	1
1	-3
2	5
3	8

Ⓒ
x	y
0	4
1	5
3	6
4	7
5	8
7	9

Ⓓ
x	y
0	1
1	2
2	4
3	6
4	8
5	10

2. Lee simplified the expression in the box. Which correct answer did Lee find?

Ⓐ $-5x$ Ⓒ $3x$

Ⓑ $-3x$ Ⓓ $5x$

Expression

$-4x - (-x)$

Name

1. Look at the equation in the box. Show your work and solve for *a*.

$$3a + 2 = a - 6$$

a = _____

2. Elton said that 10 was the value of *n* for one of the equations below. Which answer choice makes his statement true?

Ⓐ $2n + 1 = 21$

Ⓑ $2n + 2 = 21$

Ⓒ $2n + 3 = 21$

Ⓓ $2n + 4 = 21$

Name

1. Sue solved Leeroy's equation, $7x + 3 = 4x + 15$. Which correct answer did Sue give?

Ⓐ 5

Ⓑ 4

Ⓒ 3

Ⓓ 2

2. Sam is playing a video game. He had a certain number of points (*p*) when his father walked into his room. Then, Sam earned 25 more points for a total of 6,000 points. Which equation can be used to find the points (*p*) he had before his dad walked into his room?

Ⓐ $25 - p = 6,000$

Ⓑ $p - 25 = 6,000$

Ⓒ $6,000 = 25p$

Ⓓ $p + 25 = 6,000$

1. Ted and Luke checked out books from Wharton County Library. Ted read 126 pages, which was more than triple the pages Luke read. Which inequality represents this?

   Ⓐ $126 > 3L$

   Ⓑ $125 < 3L$

   Ⓒ $126 > L - 3$

   Ⓓ $125 < L + 3$

2. Robin, Terry, Lee, and Heath created tables to represent a variation between x and y. Which person did this correctly?

   Ⓐ Lee

x	y
10	20
15	30
20	40
25	50

   Ⓑ Robin

x	y
15	65
20	50
30	40
35	45

   Ⓒ Terry

x	y
1	24
2	14
3	10
4	1

   Ⓓ Heath

x	y
2	4
4	8
6	12
8	14

1. Austin wrote one of the answers below as an equivalent equation to the one Brook wrote. Which of the following is equivalent to Brook's equation?

   Ⓐ $x + 8 = 4$

   Ⓒ $24x = 4$

   Ⓑ $8 + x = 4$

   Ⓓ $4x = 8$

   > **Brook's Equation**
   >
   > $4x + 8 = 16$

2. In his mobile auto-detailing business, Lawrence charges $10 for each car he washes at a single location plus a $5 charge for supplies. Lawrence decided to lower his supplies charge to $2.50. Which equation represents the new cost for washing cars (c)?

   Ⓐ $T = 7.50c + 5.00$

   Ⓒ $T = 10c + 5.00$

   Ⓑ $T = 10c + 2.50$

   Ⓓ $T = 7.50c + 2.50$

1. Patricia is grilling steak for her husband's birthday. She purchased 36 ounces of steak to feed the 4 people in their house. At this same rate, how many ounces of steak would Patricia have to cook if her husband's parents decided to come for dinner?

Ⓐ 60 ounces

Ⓑ 54 ounces

Ⓒ 42 ounces

Ⓓ 38 ounces

2. Look at the equation in the box. What value for x makes the equation true?

$$\frac{x}{9} + 6 = 8$$

$x =$ _____

1. Doris wrote the expression $5x + 3y - 7$. She asked Sheri what the value of her expression would be if $x = -2$ and $y = 4$. If Sheri answered correctly, what answer choice did she give?

Ⓐ -10   Ⓑ -5   Ⓒ 9   Ⓓ 15

2. The table shows the relationship of values of x and y. Which of the following answer choices identifies the rule for the table?

Ⓐ $y = 2x - 1$ Ⓒ $y = x - -1$

Ⓑ $y = 2x + 1$ Ⓓ $y = x + 4$

x	y
0	-1
2	3
4	7

Name

1. Cindy is learning to type. She can type 30 words per minute. Which function gives the number of words Cindy can type (y) in x minutes?

    Ⓐ $y = \frac{1}{30}x$ Ⓒ $y = 30x$

    Ⓑ $y = 2x$ Ⓓ $y = \frac{1}{2}x$

2. For every piece of furniture Harry sells, he earns 5% commission. His commission this week is $700. What is his total value of sales?

Answer: _____

Name

1. For Teacher Appreciation Week, Wharton School District is buying gifts for their teachers. The gifts cost $4 each plus a $20 setup charge for printing. Which formula would represent the total cost for x number of gifts?

    Ⓐ $y = 4 + x + 20$ Ⓒ $y = 25x$

    Ⓑ $y = 20x + 4$ Ⓓ $y = 4x + 20$

2. Solve the problems below.

A.	B.	C.	D.
When $a = 7$,	When $d = 9$,	When $p = 4$,	When $g = 1$,
$5a + 3a =$ _____.	$d + \frac{6}{3} =$ _____.	$2(p + 5) - 9 =$ _____.	$g - 4 =$ _____.

Name

1. Look at the table below. The table shows the value in relation to the term. Complete the table.

Term	1	2	3	4	5			
Value	2	5	8	11	14			

2. Complete the table:

$y = x + 9$	
x	y
	14
2	
4	
3	

Name

1. On Saturday, Chandler went fishing with his family. He caught 9 catfish. The next day, he caught 3 catfish every hour. Which expression shows the total number of catfish Chandler caught?

Ⓐ $9 + 3h$

Ⓒ $9(3h)$

Ⓑ $9 + h$

Ⓓ $9 + 3 + h$

2. Sasha was asked to write an equation that represents the commutative property. Which correct answer choice below models this?

Ⓐ $4 \times 3 = 6 \times 2$

Ⓒ $6 \times 18 = 18 \times 6$

Ⓑ $3 + 20 = 23$

Ⓓ $10 + 3 = 7 + 6$

Name

1. Look at the table. Which expression represents the rule for the function table?

x	y
2	7
3	9
4	11
5	13

Ⓐ 5x − 3

Ⓒ 2x + 3

Ⓑ x + 5

Ⓓ 4x − 1

2. Look at the function tables. Which function table represents the equation "y is always 1 less than 2 times x"?

Ⓐ

x	y
2	3
0	1
4	7
5	9

Ⓑ

x	y
2	3
0	1
4	8
5	9

Ⓒ

x	y
2	3
0	-1
4	7
5	9

Ⓓ

x	y
2	3
0	1
4	7
5	10

Name

1. Look at the function tables. Which function table represents the equation "y is always 2 more than 3 times x"?

Ⓐ

x	y
-2	3
0	1
4	7
5	9

Ⓑ

x	y
2	3
0	1
4	8
5	9

Ⓒ

x	y
2	8
0	-2
4	14
5	17

Ⓓ

x	y
-2	-4
0	2
3	11
5	17

2. Hannah works at a local grocery store. She earns $5.50 an hour plus tips for carry-out. She worked 5 days this week for a total of h hours and earned $20 each day in tips. Which expression shows the total amount of money Hannah earned for the week?

Ⓐ 5.50h + 20

Ⓒ 5.50h(20)

Ⓑ 5.50h + (5 × 20)

Ⓓ 5.50h(5 × 20)

1. Peter repairs computers in El Campo, Texas. He charges an initial fee of $25 plus an hourly rate of $55. Which equation represents the total charge? How much would the total charge be for 6 hours of work?

Ⓐ $c = h + 25$

Ⓒ $c = 55h + 25$

Ⓑ $c = h + 55$

Ⓓ $c = 25h + 55$

6 hours = _____

2. The Sivells Elementary Booster Club is having a school carnival to earn money for new computers. The school charges $3 to attend the carnival and 50 cents for each ride (n). Which formula shows the total cost (c) for a day at the carnival for one person.

Ⓐ $c = 0.50n$

Ⓒ $c = 3n - 0.50$

Ⓑ $c = 3 + 0.50n$

Ⓓ $c = 3 + 0.50$

---

1. How can you tell if a pattern is linear?

_____

_____

_____

_____

2. Complete the function table.

$y = \frac{1}{2}x$	
x	y
-4	
-2	
0	
6	
10	

Name

Daily Warm-Up 29

1. Four students were asked to create a linear pattern. Which student did this correctly?

Ⓐ Rebecca

Ⓑ Shalle

Ⓒ Linda

Ⓓ Melissa

Melissa	(−3, −1); (−2, 0); (0, 1); (1, 2)
Linda	(2, 5); (3, 4); (4, 3); (4, 2)
Shalle	(−3, −6); (−2, −4); (−1, −2); (0, 0)
Rebecca	(2, 2); (4, 3); (5, 4); (7, 5)

2. Mary created the sequence of numbers shown below. Find the next two numbers in the sequence.

12, -4, -20, -36, ________, ________

Name

Daily Warm-Up 30

1. A teacher called Sandra to the board to simplify the problem. Help Sandra simplify the expression.

Sandra's Problem

$3y + x - 2x + y^3 + x + x$

Ⓐ $x^3 - 2x + 4y^4$

Ⓑ $x = 3y^4$

Ⓒ $5x + y + 3y$

Ⓓ $x + y^3 + 3y$

2. Michael created an expression equivalent to the one shown below. Which answer choice did Michael create?

4 • c • c + 5 + c

Ⓐ $4c^2 + c + 5$

Ⓑ $20 + c^2 + c$

Ⓒ $9c + c^2$

Ⓓ $7c + 5$

Name

1. Simplify the expression:

$$3x^2 + 3x - x^2 + 5 + 5x$$

2. Sue worked out a step in an equation below and ended up with $3x + 7 - 7 = 16 - 7$. Which equation is she trying to solve?

Ⓐ $3x + 7 = 16$

Ⓒ $16 - 7x + 3 = 3$

Ⓑ $3x + 7 = 16 - 7$

Ⓓ $3x + 7 = 16 - 7$

Name

1. Use the given rule to find the missing values.

Rule $y = x - 4$	
x	y
18	
14	
17	
1	

2. Use the given rules to find the missing values below.

A.

Rule $y = 3x - 2$	
x	y
0	
3	
7	
6	

B.

Rule $y = 6x + 4$	
x	y
	28
	88
	76
	58

1. Michael wrote the equation on the board. Solve for *a*.

$$\frac{a}{6} - 3 = 12$$

a = _____

2. Show the algebraic steps necessary to solve the equation in the box.

$$\frac{x}{3} + 5 = 8$$

x = _____

1. Solve the equations below. (Be sure to show your algebraic steps to solving the problems.)

A. $5a + 25 = 75$ **B.** $3x + 7 = 28$

a = _____   *x* = _____

2. A teacher asked four students to create a pattern of numbers that increased by 4. Which student did this correctly?

Ⓐ Amber   Ⓒ Jennifer

Ⓑ Karen   Ⓓ Natalie

Student	Pattern
Natalie	2, -1, 3, 7
Jennifer	0, -4, -8, -12
Karen	-5, -1, 3, 7
Amber	0, 2, 4, 6

1. Look at the table. Which rule best describes the value of *n* in terms of the value of *m*? Fill in the missing numbers on the table and write the rule below.

m	2	3	4	5	6	7
n	14	23				

Rule: _____

2. Brodie is making a deck for his back yard. To complete the project, he realized he would need 2 more boards. He went to the lumberyard and bought both boards that had a combined length of $5\frac{3}{4}$ feet. The first board was $1\frac{1}{4}$ feet long and the second board had a measurement of *x*. Write an equation to represent the lengths of the two boards. How long was the second board?

Equation: _____

x = _____

1. At a grocery store, the ratio of soda to other drinks sold is 4:1. If there were a total of 944 sodas sold, how many other drinks were sold at the grocery store?

Answer: _____

2. During the summer months, the ratio of people swimming at Aquatic Center on Saturdays to Sundays was 3 to 7. Which shows the number of swimmers on Saturday and Sunday that could have been at the Aquatic Center over the weekend?

Ⓐ 24 Saturday swimmers and 49 Sunday swimmers

Ⓑ 21 Saturday swimmers and 36 Sunday swimmers

Ⓒ 9 Saturday swimmers and 14 Sunday swimmers

Ⓓ 21 Saturday swimmers and 49 Sunday swimmers

1. Carrie created the expression below for her sister to simplify. Which correct answer choice did her sister give?

$$3a + 6b - 7a - (-3b) + 9c$$

Ⓐ $-4a + 9b + 9c$

Ⓒ $4a + 3b + 9c$

Ⓑ $4a - 3b - 9c$

Ⓓ $-4a - 3b + 9c$

2. Jennie created the expression below. Which of the answer choices below is a simplified form of the expression Jennie created?

Ⓐ $7x - 8$

Ⓒ $-7x + 8$

Ⓑ $7x + 8$

Ⓓ $-7x - 8$

Jennie's Expression
$-3x + 8 + 10x$

---

1. Jack and Henry are cousins. Jack is trying to create an equation to represent both their ages. He knows that Henry is 5 years younger than twice Jack's age (j). If Henry is 15 years old (h), how old is Jack (j)? Write an equation and solve for j.

Equation: _____ $j =$ _____

2. Four students were asked to create an equation that results in $k = 8$. According to the table, which student did *not* do this correctly?

Ⓐ Martha

Ⓒ Jim

Ⓑ Peggy

Ⓓ Sherry

Student	Equation
Sherry	$2k - 3k = -8$
Jim	$6k + 3k = 72$
Martha	$7k + k = 56$
Peggy	$10k - 2k = 64$

Name

1. Stan worked at his grandfather's store on the weekend. On Saturday, he earned $57.75 for 7 hours of work. At this rate, how much will he earn if he works 9 hours on Sunday?

Answer: _____

2. Mitchell created a pattern and asked his friend to choose which rule applies to his pattern. His friend answered correctly. Which answer choice did Mitchell's friend pick?

Ⓐ numbers are increased by 6

Ⓑ 3 is multiplied by factors increased by 1

Ⓒ exponents of 3 are increased by 1

Ⓓ 3 is added to the existing number

Mitchell's Pattern

3, 9, 27, 81

Name

1. A teacher created the function table below and asked her students to create an equation in which c represents the cost of an object and n represents the quantity bought. Four students raised their hands, and the teacher called on each person for an answer. Which student created a correct equation?

Ⓐ Betty: $c = 6n + 1$ Ⓒ Norman: $c = 10n - 3$

Ⓑ Norma: $c = 5n + 2$ Ⓓ James: $c = 7n$

n	c
1	7
2	12
3	17
4	22

2. Lisa created an input-output table with the rule $f(x) = 3x + 3$. If -2 was put into the input, what would be the output number?

Ⓐ 0   Ⓑ 2   Ⓒ 3   Ⓓ -3

Name

1. A teacher created an input-output table with the rule for the equation $f(x) = 2x - 2$. If -3 was put into the input, what would be the output number?

Answer: _____

2. Stu has 3 more than 2 times as many green marbles as Gene. If Gene has n marbles, which expression represents the number of marbles Stu has?

Ⓐ $3(n + 3)$

Ⓑ $2n + 3$

Ⓒ $2n + 5$

Ⓓ $3n + 2$

Name

1. Look at the table below. Complete the table by multiplying the term by 3 then subtracting 2.

Term	1	2	3	4	5	6	7
Number	1						

2. Four groups of students were asked to create an equivalent expression to the one the teacher wrote on the board. Which group did this correctly?

Ⓐ Group 1   Ⓒ Group 3

Ⓑ Group 2   Ⓓ Group 4

Teacher's Expression $5(a + a + b)$	
Group	**Expression**
1	$10a + b$
2	$5a + 5b$
3	$15ab$
4	$10a + 5b$

Name

1. June's homework assignment is to find an expression equivalent to $2(4x - 3y) + 3(2x + 4y)$. If June does this correctly, which answer choice below is an equivalent form?

Ⓐ $14x - 2y$

Ⓑ $14x + 6y$

Ⓒ $14x - y$

Ⓓ $14x - 3y$

2. Simplify the two expressions below to find equivalent forms.

A. $4(2x - 2y) + 3(4x + 2y)$ B. $2(6x - 2x) + 6(3x + 4y)$

Name

1. Marsha and Allie are debating who's right or wrong on the problem $-2(3 - x) = 4(2x - 5)$. Marsha thinks $x = \frac{7}{6}$, but Allie thinks the answer is $x = \frac{7}{3}$. Work on the problem to find who is right.

Answer: _____

2. Henry is a carpenter. For each job, he charges $150 for equipment and $45 for each hour ($h$) he works. Which expression below represents the total amount of money Henry charges for each job?

Ⓐ $150 + 45(45 + h)$ Ⓒ $(150 + 45)h$

Ⓑ $150 + 45h$ Ⓓ $150h + 25h$

Name

1. A teacher called Mike to the board to simplify the expression below. If Mike got the answer correct, which answer choice below did he choose?

$$(62 - 24) \cdot \sqrt{16}$$

Ⓐ 4   Ⓑ 16   Ⓒ 152   Ⓓ 108

2. Cody is power-washing his home. At a local parts store, he can rent a power washer. The cost includes a one-time rental fee of $25 and $12.50 for each hour. The table below shows the relationship between the number of hours Cody rented the power washer and the total cost of the rental. Complete the table by calculating the total cost for the numbers of hours rented.

Hours	1	2	3	4	5	6	7	8
Cost	$37.50	$	$	$	$	$	$	$

Name

1. Christi is creating a geometric pattern with numbers. Based on Christi's pattern, what would be the two remaining numbers in her pattern?

$7^1 = 7$ $7^2 = 49$ $7^3 = 343$ _____ = _____   _____ = _____

2. Complete the function tables below.

A.

$y = 2x$	
x	**y**
6	12
9	18
4	
7	

B.

$y = 4x - 2$	
x	**y**
5	18
7	
	38
4	

Name _____

1. Complete the table. Explain what is happening and how to get the output number.

_____

_____

_____

_____

Input (m)	Output (x)
1	
3	
5	
7	
$x = 3m - 4$	

2. Complete the table. Explain what is happening and how to get the output number.

_____

_____

_____

_____

Input (m)	Output (7)
1	
2	
3	
4	
$y = 5m + 4$	

Name _____

1. Which table represents the equation correctly?

Ⓐ
$y = 3x + 1$	
x	**y**
0	1
1	4
2	5
3	9
4	11

Ⓑ
$y = 3x + 1$	
x	**y**
0	1
1	3
2	7
3	8
4	13

Ⓒ
$y = 3x + 1$	
x	**y**
0	2
1	5
2	8
3	11
4	134

Ⓓ
$y = 3x + 1$	
x	**y**
0	1
1	4
2	7
3	10
4	13

2. Beverly was asked to evaluate the expression $2(33 - 6) + 2$. If she found the answer, what correct answer did she give?

Answer: _____

Name

1. Mr. Kearny used the expression $2x + 4$ to determine the number of chairs he needed for his science lab. If x is the number of tables in the science lab, how many chairs should he order for his science lab if there are 12 tables?

Answer: _____

2. At the beginning of school, a teacher in a geometry class defined the term *equation*. What is a definition of *equation*?

_____

_____

_____

_____

Name

1. Jack wrote the equation $4x = 28$. Which type of situation is best represented by the equation Jack wrote?

Ⓐ Four brothers went to the movies, and when they divided the bill evenly, x is the amount each brother paid.

Ⓑ Four brothers went to the movies and each paid $28 to get in.

Ⓒ Four brothers went to the movies and only 2 paid for all 4 to get in.

Ⓓ not given

2. Examine the patterns below. Which number pattern below matches the rule that each number is 5 less than 3 times the previous number?

Ⓐ 3 7 19 55   Ⓒ 2 4 6 12

Ⓑ 3 4 7 16   Ⓓ 3 7 21 55

Name

1. Greg created the expression shown below. Use the order of operations to simplify Greg's equation.

Ⓐ -63

Ⓑ 6

Ⓒ 23

Ⓓ 210

$$5 + 42 - (22 \times 5)$$

2. Braxton was asked by his teacher to go to the board and simplify the expression below. If Braxton did this correctly, which answer did he give?

Ⓐ $2x - 2x^2$

Ⓑ $2x^2 + 2x$

Ⓒ $6x - 9x^2$

Ⓓ $5x + x^2$

$$9x - 11x + 2x^2 + 4x$$

Name

1. Wanda was asked by her teacher to go to the board and solve the problem she wrote. What should Wanda do first?

Ⓐ Add 8 to both sides.

Ⓑ Subtract 8 from both sides.

Ⓒ Subtract 24 from both sides.

Ⓓ Multiply both sides by 3.

$$\frac{x}{3} - 8 = 24$$

2. Hamon's homework assignment is to identify the rule for the pattern below. Which answer choice below is the correct rule?

5	-25	125	-625	3,125	-15,625

Ⓐ Add 20 to the previous number.

Ⓑ The numbers are multiplied by 5.

Ⓒ The numbers are multiplied by -5.

Ⓓ The numbers are increasing by 20.

Name

1. Find the solution to the equation.

$$5x + 26 = 44$$

x = _____

2. Look at the equation below. What is the value of x?

$$\frac{x}{4} - 4 = 20$$

x = _____

Name

1. Jenny created the equation below for her brother to solve. If her brother solved the equation correctly, what value for m makes the equation true?

Ⓐ $\frac{21}{25}$ Ⓒ $\frac{9}{25}$

Ⓑ $\frac{17}{50}$ Ⓓ $\frac{33}{50}$

$$m - \frac{4}{25} = \frac{1}{2}$$

2. Use the key to solve this expression: $\frac{1}{2}y - x$

Key:

x	y
5	-2

Answer: _____

1. Complete the function table by following the given rule.

$y = 3(x - 2)$	
x	**y**
3	
6	
	21
	33

2. Simplify the problem below.

$$4x^5(9x^3)$$

Answer: _____

1. Complete the function table by following the given rule.

$y = 4(x - 2)$	
x	**y**
4	
	16
8	
	32

2. Simplify the problem below.

$$(9x)(3x^2y)$$

Answer: _____

1. Simplify the problem below.

$$(2x)(4x^3y)$$

Answer: _____

2. Simplify the problem below.

$$(5x^2y^4)(7x^5y)$$

Answer: _____

1. What is a non-linear pattern?

_____

_____

_____

_____

2. A teacher wrote a sequence of numbers on the board and asked her students what she should do to find the next number in the pattern. If her students answered correctly, which choice identifies the answer they gave?

$$\boxed{0, 4, 12, 28, 60, 124}$$

Ⓐ Add 4 to the previous number.

Ⓒ Add 4 to the previous number then multiply by 2.

Ⓑ Add 2 to the previous number then multiply by 2.

Ⓓ Add 2 to the previous number then multiply by 4.

1. Pete needs to find an expression equivalent to the one shown below. Which answer choice is the correct answer?

Ⓐ $2x^2 - 2x + 20$

Ⓒ $2x^2 - 4x + 13$

Ⓑ $6x^2 + 13$

Ⓓ $4x^2 + 20$

$$x + 7 - 3x + 2x^2 + 13$$

2. Liz and Sandra love making bracelets. Liz has b number of bracelets. Sandra has 3 more than 3 times the number of bracelets Liz has. Which expression can be used to determine the number of bracelets Sandra has?

Ⓐ $3 + b$

Ⓑ $3b + 3$

Ⓒ $3b + 3b$

Ⓓ $b + 3 + 3$

1. Student 1 wrote the expression 3(43) and student 2 wrote 12 × 12 × 12. Did these two students write problems with the same value? Explain.

_____

_____

_____

_____

2. Which answer choice identifies what is happening in the function table?

Ⓐ $t = 2n + 1$

Ⓑ $t = 3n - 1$

Ⓒ $t = 2n - 1$

Ⓓ $t = 3n + 2$

Number (n)	1	2	3	4	5
Term (t)	★ ★ ★	★ ★ ★ ★ ★	★ ★ ★ ★ ★ ★ ★	★ ★ ★ ★ ★ ★ ★ ★ ★	★ ★ ★ ★ ★ ★ ★ ★ ★ ★ ★

1. Maci wrote a rule to describe the table Ty created. What correct rule did Maci write?

Ⓐ $y = 8x + 3$

Ⓑ $y = 8x + 4$

Ⓒ $y = 8x - 2$

Ⓓ $y = 8x - 4$

x	y
5	36
6	44
7	52
8	60
9	68

2. Brandi runs track at school. Today, she ran 3 miles. Kendall, Brandi's younger cousin, asked her how many feet are in 3 miles. Which of the following can be used to find y, the number of feet, in 3 miles?

Ⓐ $y = 3 \times 5,280$

Ⓑ $y = 5,280/3$

Ⓒ $y = 3 \times 1,760$

Ⓓ $y = 1,760/3$

1. Which expression shown below has a value of -4?

Ⓐ $-8 - (4)$

Ⓑ $-8 - (-4)$

Ⓒ $-4 - (8)$

Ⓓ $-4 - (-8)$

2. Chandler told Ty he was thinking of a number. He told Ty that the sum of his number (n) and $29 = 84$. Solve for n to find Chandler's number.

Answer: _____

Warm-Up 1
1. B   2. 450 students

Warm-Up 2
1. $42   2. B

Warm-Up 3
1. D   2. D; $n = 53$

Warm-Up 4
1. C   2. $x = -18$

Warm-Up 5
1. B   2. A

Warm-Up 6
1. 8 bow ties   2. D

Warm-Up 7
1. B   2. C

Warm-Up 8
1. D;

Tickets Sold	Money Raised
4	$248
7	$434
10	$620
15	$930

2. x = # of books
y = time it takes to reshelve

x	y
5	11
25	31
35	41
45	51

Warm-Up 9
1. $30a - 34$ 2. D; $n = 23$

Warm-Up 10
1. D   2. $18a - 9b$

Warm-Up 11
1. B   2. D

Warm-Up 12
1. D   2. C

Warm-Up 13
1. B   2. Bella

Warm-Up 14
1. A   2. B

Warm-Up 15
1. $a = -4$ 2. A

Warm-Up 16
1. B   2. D

Warm-Up 17
1. A   2. A

Warm-Up 18
1. D   2. B

Warm-Up 19
1. B   2. $x = 18$

Warm-Up 20
1. B   2. A

Warm-Up 21
1. C   2. $14,000

Warm-Up 22
1. D
2. A. 56   B. 11   C. 9   D. -3

Warm-Up 23
1.

Term	1	2	3	4	5	6	7	8
Value	2	5	8	11	14	17	20	23

2. $y = x + 9$

x	y
5	14
2	11
4	13
3	12

Warm-Up 24
1. A   2. C

Warm-Up 25
1. C   2. C

Warm-Up 26
1. D   2. B

Warm-Up 27
1. C;   2. B
6 hours = $355

Warm-Up 28
1. If the numbers are arranged following the same rule and forms a straight line when graphed, it's a linear pattern. If the pattern changes, it's non-linear.
2. -2, -1, 0, 3, 5

Warm-Up 29
1. B   2. -52, -68

Warm-Up 30
1. D   2. A

Warm-Up 31
1. $2x^2 + 8x + 5$ 2. A

Warm-Up 32
1.

Rule $y = x - 4$	
x	y
18	14
14	10
17	13
1	-3

2. A.

Rule $y = 3x - 2$	
x	y
0	-2
3	7
7	19
6	16

B.

Rule $y = 6x + 4$	
x	y
4	28
14	88
12	76
9	58

Warm-Up 33
1. $a = 90$ 2. $x = 9$

Warm-Up 34
1. A. $a = 10$, B. $x = 7$ 2. B

Warm-Up 35
1. Rule: $9m - 4$

m	2	3	4	5	6	7
n	14	23	32	41	50	59

2. $1\frac{1}{4} + x = 5\frac{3}{4}$ ft. $x = 4\frac{1}{2}$ ft.

Warm-Up 36
1. 236 drinks   2. D

Warm-Up 37
1. A   2. B

Warm-Up 38
1. $2j - 5 = 15$, $j = 10$ 2. A

Warm-Up 39
1. $74.25   2. C

Warm-Up 40
1. B   2. D

Warm-Up 41
1. -8   2. B

Warm-Up 42
1.

Term	1	2	3	4	5	6	7
Number	1	4	7	10	13	16	19

2. D

Warm-Up 43
1. B
2. A. $20x - 2y$
    B. $26x + 24y$

Warm-Up 44
1. Allie: $x = \frac{7}{3}$ 2. B

Warm-Up 45
1. C
2.

Hours	1	2	3	4	5	6	7	8
Cost	$37.50	$50.00	$62.50	$75.00	$87.50	$100.00	$112.50	$125.00

Warm-Up 46
1. $7^4 = 2,401$ and $7^5 = 16,807$
2. A.

x	y
6	12
9	18
4	8
7	14

B.

x	y
5	18
7	26
10	38
4	14

Warm-Up 47
1. Multiply the input by 3 and subtract 4.

Input (m)	Output (x)
1	-1
3	5
5	11
7	17
$x = 3m - 4$	

2. Multiply the input by 5 and add 4.

Input (m)	Output (y)
1	9
2	14
3	19
4	24
$y = 5m + 4$	

Warm-Up 48
1. D   2. 56

Warm-Up 49
1. 28 chairs
2. An equation is a mathematical statement in which two mathematical expressions are equal.

Warm-Up 50
1. A   2. B

Warm-Up 51
1. A   2. B

Warm-Up 52
1. A   2. C

Warm-Up 53
1. $x = 3.6$ 2. $x = 96$

Warm-Up 54
1. D   2. -6

Warm-Up 55
1.

$y = 3(x - 9)$	
x	y
3	3
6	12
9	21
13	33

2. $36x^8$

Warm-Up 56
1.

$y = 4(x - 2)$	
x	y
4	8
6	16
8	24
10	32

2. $27x^3y$

Warm-Up 57
1. $8x^4y$ 2. $35x^7y^5$

Warm-Up 58
1. A pattern is non-linear when there are varying rates of change and it does not form a straight line when graphed.
2. B

Warm-Up 59
1. A   2. B

Warm-Up 60
1. No; $3(43) = 129$ and $12 \times 12 \times 12 = 1,728$
2. A

Warm-Up 61
1. D   2. A

Warm-Up 62
1. B   2. $n = 55$